Advanced Introduction to the Law of International Organizations

Elgar Advanced Introductions are stimulating and thoughtful introductions to major fields in the social sciences and law, expertly written by the world's leading scholars. Designed to be accessible yet rigorous, they offer concise and lucid surveys of the substantive and policy issues associated with discrete subject areas.

The aims of the series are two-fold: to pinpoint essential principles of a particular field, and to offer insights that stimulate critical thinking. By distilling the vast and often technical corpus of information on the subject into a concise and meaningful form, the books serve as accessible introductions for undergraduate and graduate students coming to the subject for the first time. Importantly, they also develop well-informed, nuanced critiques of the field that will challenge and extend the understanding of advanced students, scholars and policy-makers.

Titles in the series include:

International Political Economy
Benjamin J. Cohen

The Austrian School of Economics
Randall G. Holcombe

Cultural Economics
Ruth Towse

Law and Development
*Michael J. Trebilcock and Mariana
Mota Prado*

International Humanitarian Law
Robert Kolb

International Tax Law
Reuven S. Avi-Yonah

Post Keynesian Economics
J.E. King

International Conflict and Security Law
Nigel D. White

Comparative Constitutional Law
Mark Tushnet

International Human Rights Law
Dinah L. Shelton

Entrepreneurship
Robert D. Hisrich

International Trade Law
Michael J. Trebilcock

Public Policy
B. Guy Peters

The Law of International Organizations
Jan Klabbers

Advanced Introduction to

The Law of International Organizations

JAN KLABBERS

Academy Professor, Erik Castrén Institute, Faculty of Law, University of Helsinki, Finland

Elgar Advanced Introductions

Edward Elgar
PUBLISHING

Cheltenham, UK • Northampton, MA, USA

Published by
Edward Elgar Publishing Limited
The Lypiatts
15 Lansdown Road
Cheltenham
Glos GL50 2JA
UK

Edward Elgar Publishing, Inc.
William Pratt House
9 Dewey Court
Northampton
Massachusetts 01060
USA

A catalogue record for this book
is available from the British Library

Library of Congress Control Number: 2015935883

ISBN 978 1 78254 094 6 (cased)
ISBN 978 1 78254 427 2 (paperback)
ISBN 978 1 78254 095 3 (eBook)

Typeset by Servis Filmsetting Ltd, Stockport, Cheshire
Printed and bound in Great Britain by T.J. International Ltd, Padstow

Contents

Preface

The aim of this book is to provide an introductory overview of the basic legal structures that together make up the operating system of the institutions through which much global governance is exercised: international (or intergovernmental) organizations. Moreover, the book aims to do so by placing the law in (political) context; it hopes to help the reader in understanding how the law works and why it works the way it does, without going into much detail on the contents of international institutional law.

Global executive power emanates from entities such as the UN, the World Bank, or the World Trade Organization: decisions taken by these bodies can potentially affect the everyday lives of billions of people. Something similar holds true on a regional level with respect to such entities as the European Union or, to a lesser extent, the African Union or the Organization of American States. Hence, in order to understand (global) governance and try and keep it under control, it might prove useful to provide a basic overview of how such entities operate, whether there are limits to what they can legally do, and how (if at all) they can be controlled.

Given its format, this book necessarily paints with broad strokes. This entails that it is not very suitable as a university level textbook on international institutional law.[1] Future international legal professionals may be expected to display knowledge on a level of detail deeper than this book provides, but for the informed citizen this book may help her or him to come to reasoned opinions on the United Nations'

---

1 Other books are far more suitable for such a purpose. See, for example, Jan Klabbers, *An Introduction to International Organizations Law* (3rd edn, forthcoming); C.F. Amerasinghe, *Principles of the Institutional Law of International Organizations* (2nd edn, 2005); Philippe Sands and Pierre Klein, *Bowett's Law of International Institutions* (6th edn, 2009); and the encyclopedic H.G. Schermers and Niels M. Blokker, *International Institutional Law: Unity Within Diversity* (5th edn, 2011). Not a textbook in the traditional sense, but very useful is Evelyne Lagrange and Jean-Marc Sorel (eds.), *Traité de droit des organisations internationales* (2013).

latest enterprise, or how to assess the activities of the World Trade Organization, or the most recent policing engagement of the North Atlantic Treaty Organization.

No book is written in a vacuum, and that holds for this one too. Having thought, taught, written and spoken (not necessarily always in this order) about international institutional law for close to two decades, I have accumulated many intellectual debts to a great number of individuals, both within international organizations and academia. They are too numerous to mention here, and their contributions to my thinking have been too isolated and incidental to even reconstruct with any precision who has contributed what exactly. The main, and identifiable if often intangible contribution, has been made by my wife Margareta and my children Johan and Gilda. It is to them that this book is dedicated.

Abbreviations

ANZUS	Australia, New Zealand, United States Security Treaty
ARIO	Articles on the Responsibility of International Organizations
ASEAN	Association of South East Asian Nations
AU	African Union
BIS	Bank for International Settlements
BRICS	Brazil, Russia, India, China, South Africa
CJEU	Court of Justice of the European Union
COMECON	Council for Mutual Economic Assistance
EBRD	European Bank for Reconstruction and Development
ECHR	European Convention on Human Rights
ECR	European Court Reports
ECSC	European Coal and Steel Community
ECtHR	European Court of Human Rights
EEC	European Economic Community
EFTA	European Free Trade Area
EP	European Parliament
EU	European Union
EUI	European University Institute
FAO	Food and Agriculture Organization
FYROM	Former Yugoslav Republic of Macedonia
GAL	Global Administrative Law
GATT	General Agreement on Tariffs and Trade
GEF	Global Environmental Facility
IAEA	International Atomic Energy Agency
ICAO	International Civil Aviation Organization
ICJ	International Court of Justice
ICSID	International Centre for the Settlement of Investment Disputes
ICTR	International Criminal Tribunal for Rwanda
ICTY	International Criminal Tribunal for Former Yugoslavia
IDA	International Development Association

IFAD	International Fund for Agricultural Development
IFC	International Finance Corporation
ILA	International Law Association
ILC	International Law Commission
ILO	International Labour Organization
ILOAT	ILO Administrative Tribunal
ILR	International Law Reports
IMCO	Intergovernmental Maritime Consultative Organization
IMF	International Monetary Fund
IMO	International Maritime Organization
IOM	International Organization for Migration
ITIO	International Trade and Investment Organization
ITU	International Telecommunication Union
MIGA	Multilateral Investment Guarantee Agency
MoU	Memorandum of Understanding
NATO	North Atlantic Treaty Organization
NGO	non-governmental organization
nyr	not yet reported
OAS	Organization of American States
OAU	Organization of African Unity
OECD	Organisation for Economic Co-operation and Development
OIC	Organization of Islamic Cooperation
OPCW	Organization for the Prohibition of Chemical Weapons
OPEC	Organization of Petroleum Exporting Countries
OSCE	Organization for Security and Cooperation in Europe
PCIJ	Permanent Court of International Justice
TEU	Treaty on European Union
TFEU	Treaty on the Functioning of the European Union
UK	United Kingdom
UN	United Nations
UNCLOS	United Nations Convention on the Law of the Sea
UNCTAD	United Nations Conference on Trade and Development
UNDP	United Nations Development Programme
UNEP	United Nations Environment Programme
UNESCO	United Nations Organization for Education, Science and Culture
UNHCR	United Nations High Commissioner for Refugees
UNICEF	United Nations Children's Fund
UNIDO	United Nations Industrial Development Organization

UPOV	International Union for the Protection of New Varieties of Plants
UPU	Universal Postal Union
US	United States
VCLT	Vienna Convention on the Law of Treaties
WFP	World Food Programme
WHO	World Health Organization
WIPO	World Intellectual Property Organization
WMO	World Meteorological Organization
WTO	World Trade Organization

Table of cases

Permanent Court of Justice/International Court of Justice

Court of Justice of the European Union

Others

1 The concept of international organization

1.1 Introduction

International organizations help to shape the world we live in. The world would be a different place (and probably far worse) without the peacekeepers of the United Nations (UN), without the vaccination passports and health regulations of the World Health Organization (WHO), without the emergency food being provided by the World Food Programme (WFP), or the help offered to individuals in need by the UN High Commissioner for Refugees (UNHCR). The world would also be a different place without the free trade sponsored and monitored by the World Trade Organization (WTO), the conditional loans offered by the International Monetary Fund (IMF), or the financial regulations of the Basel Committee. And the world could well be a different place if only there were more systematic and comprehensive global financial regulation, or if environmental protection went deeper than the efforts of the United Nations Environment Programme (UNEP).

International organizations coordinate efforts of states on issues of international relevance. It goes without saying that deadly diseases do not stop at national borders; hence WHO. It goes without saying that people persecuted for their religious or political beliefs should be able to find a free haven elsewhere; hence UNHCR. And it goes without saying that delivery of mail at fixed rates across boundaries is useful and agreeable; hence the Universal Postal Union (UPU). These examples suggest that international organizations (or at least some of them) are devoted to the common good in a non-offensive way. However, other examples are less politically innocent. While it is no doubt a good thing that impoverished states can receive loans and support from the IMF, many have expressed serious doubts about both the efficiency and the morality of the IMF's adjustment policies. While the free trade overseen by the WTO may generally be a good thing, many have expressed concerns about prioritizing trade over, say, human rights, or environmental protection. And while many heralded the North Atlantic Treaty Organization's (NATO) role as a defensive alliance, possibly preventing the Cold War from heating up, NATO's subsequent activities as a self-proclaimed global police force active in places like Kosovo and Afghanistan have understandably raised some eyebrows.

International organizations are creatures of modernity.[1] The first serious wave of creating them came in the wake of the industrial revolution; coincided with both the scramble for Africa and the birth of the United States (US) as a colonial power; and accompanied a rock-solid belief in science and rationality. The underlying sentiment held that the world could be controlled and organized if it could be captured in hard data. These were the days when Esperanto was created: a global language. And not coincidentally, these were the days when many international organizations started to see the light of day: telegraphic traffic became organized around standard rates in what was then the International Telegraph Union (later renamed International Telecommunication Union (ITU)); postal traffic became organized in UPU; measures became standardized with the help of the International Bureau for Weights and Measures; and in the aftermath of the industrial revolution, it stood to reason to protect intellectual property across borders (the Berne Union, forerunner of today's World Intellectual Property Organization (WIPO)).

In addition, difficult political situations were subjected to international governance, with greater or lesser success. This already started earlier in the nineteenth century, with the creation of the Rhine Commission and, following the Crimean war in the mid-nineteenth century, the Danube Commission. Some of the more successful initiatives included the financing of a lighthouse on the Moroccan coast, at Cape Spartel. Some of these were also outright failures, such as attempts to establish international governance over Albania in the early twentieth century. And some attempts were downright curious, none more so perhaps than the attempt to set up an international organization for colonialism.[2]

---

1 A useful historical overview is Bob Reinalda, *Routledge History of International Organizations: From 1815 to the Present Day* (2009); a fine discussion of the development of the underlying idea is Mark Mazower, *Governing the World: The History of an Idea* (2012); while an excellent neo-Gramscian account of the development of international organizations is offered by Craig N. Murphy, *International Organization and Industrial Change: Global Governance since 1850* (1994).

2 This was discussed with considerable enthusiasm in Edouard Baron Descamps, *Les offices internationaux et leur avenir* (1894), 38–41.

If the attempt to set up an organization for colonialism was aborted, nonetheless colonialism played an important role in the formation of the theory surrounding international organizations. International lawyers started to give serious thought to these creatures around the turn of the twentieth century, with a few articles by Odessa-based law professor Pierre Kazansky paving the way.[3] The decisive impetus, however, for what became known as functionalism, resides in the work of an American scholar and diplomat, Paul S. Reinsch.[4] Reinsch was the first to devote systematic attention to how organizations worked, and theorized that they were all set up to perform specific functions. These functions would, by and large, be technical, non-political, and thus could not be considered harmful: think of regulating postal traffic. By performing these functions, organizations would contribute to the global good: they would help make the world ready for peace, on the underlying thought that if nations cooperate with each other, they will have less incentive to go to war. Hence, organizations are a force for good, and consequently, the law should facilitate and stimulate them. As a result, international organizations would come to enjoy immunities from prosecution and taxation, and would be able to do not just the tasks that were explicitly delegated to them, but also tasks that might be related to their mandates in different ways.

While Reinsch was by no means an imperialist, he did think that colonialism could be a force for good: colonialism was one way for states to cooperate to mutual advantage. As such, it was no different from having trade relations, or, indeed, from setting up an international organization. These were all manifestations of the same impulse: to cooperate across borders for the greater good of mankind. Much of Reinsch's methodology was borrowed from the way he had conducted studies of colonialism prior to his writings on international organizations. Many insights were gained on the basis of a comparison across institutions or situations, and at times he literally equated colonial domination and international organizations, for instance when endorsing the virtues of the Union of American Republics to a sceptical audience at the Milwaukee Banker's Association, in 1906. Here, Reinsch explicitly pointed out that for the US, it would be good

---

3 See for example, Pierre Kazansky, "Théorie de l'administration internationale", (1902) 9 *Revue Générale de Droit International Public* 352–66.

4 See in particular Paul S. Reinsch, *Public International Unions, Their Work and Organization: A Study in International Administrative Law* (1911). For an exploration of the relevance of Reinsch's work, see Jan Klabbers, "The Emergence of Functionalism in International Institutional Law: Colonial Inspirations", (2014) 25 *European Journal of International Law* 645–75.

to establish cooperation with the rest of the Americas, and it literally did not matter much whether that cooperation were set up in the form of colonial ties or in the form of an international organization – the net result would be the same: a form of cooperation, mutually beneficial, and dominated by the US.

With his writings, Reinsch established the dominant theory of the law of international organizations: the theory of functionalism. This was further consolidated, expanded and, arguably, killed off, just before the setting up of the League of Nations, by a short book written by the son-in-law of US president Woodrow Wilson, the driving force behind the League.[5] In this book, Francis B. (Frank) Sayre further consolidated functionalist thought by pointing out that organizations could be successful if based on a functional need and if driven by a powerful member state, or a small group of powerful member states. Therewith, Sayre too made clear (however unwittingly) how international cooperation could be difficult to distinguish from colonial domination.[6]

One other feature of Sayre's book, however, was his radical expansion of the notion of international organization. Reinsch had, without being rigidly systematic, an intuitive sense that only those entities that work for the common good should be seen as proper international organizations. Sayre, however, happily included all forms of international cooperation in his concept of international organization. Where Reinsch had viewed the Cape Spartel lighthouse as an entity on the fringes, for Sayre it was a fine example of an organization. Where Reinsch only discussed the various river commissions with hesitations, Sayre wholeheartedly embraced them as examples of international organizations. For him, well-nigh all forms of international cooperation could qualify as such: he only drew the line, and even then with palpable regret, at the condominium established by France and the UK over the New Hebrides. This, he suggested, was no longer an international organization proper, but well-nigh everything else could be included.

Sayre's approach might seem an innocent game of academic classification, as interesting to ordinary people as ornithology is to birds, but turned out to be of enormous relevance. In treating all kinds of

---

5 The creation of the League of Nations and the ILO immediately after the Second World War is often seen as symbolizing a "move to institutions". See David Kennedy, "The Move to Institutions", (1987) 8 *Cardozo Law Review* 841–988.

6 See Francis B. Sayre, *Experiments in International Administration* (1919).

ventures as international organizations, he accomplished (however unwittingly) two things. First, he legitimized them politically. Viewing the river commissions in China as international organizations rather than as exercises in Western imperialism, helped to make these commissions seem acceptable. Second, by classifying all these entities as international organizations, he also paved the way for them to be granted the legal status and benefits that flow from that status. In particular, there is a strong assumption that international organizations are entitled to privileges and immunities. The precise scope thereof may be subject to negotiations with their host states, but the entitlement as such is undoubted. Hence, Sayre's approach turned out to be of the utmost relevance.[7]

If organizations were creatures of modernity, the Second World War once again suggested, by default, that international cooperation was a bare necessity. The outbreak of the war had been attributed by many to national egotism, and the only way to overcome this was to establish all kinds of forms of cooperation, be it on the global level or on the regional level, and in all possible issue areas. Hence, the UN was created in the ashes of the League of Nations, and organizations were set up devoted to monetary issues (the IMF), reconstruction and development (the World Bank), education and culture (the UN Organization for Education, Science and Culture (UNESCO)), food and agriculture (the Food and Agriculture Organization (FAO)), health (the WHO), trade (General Agreement on Tariffs and Trade, in other words, GATT, now the WTO), maritime relations (Intergovernmental Maritime Consultative Organization (IMCO), now the International Maritime Organization (IMO)), aviation (International Civil Aviation Organization (ICAO)) and many more. Some of these had had early forerunners: the FAO grew out of the International Institute for Agriculture, first established in 1905, while the WHO consolidated and brought together various regional forms of cooperation in the health sector.

On the regional level, too, organizations mushroomed. In Europe alone, the immediate postwar period saw the creation of Benelux, the Council of Europe, NATO (involving also Canada and the US) and, most spectacularly, the European Union (EU). In Latin America, the Organization of American States (OAS) became the reincarnation of

---

7 See in much greater detail Jan Klabbers, "The EJIL Foreword: The Transformation of International Organizations Law", (2015) 26 *European Journal of International Law* 9–82.

the earlier Union of American Republics, and the newly independent states of Africa set up the Organization of African Unity (OAU) in the early 1960s (now the African Union (AU)). In Asia, the degree of international organization was less marked, with the Association of South East Asian Nations (ASEAN) being limited to a rather loose form of cooperation.

Today's organizational landscape sees a great variety, from universal and regional organizations to organizations devoted to specific cultures (for example, the Organisation international de la francophonie) and specific commodities such as oil (Organization of Petroleum Exporting Countries (OPEC)), but also coffee, cocoa, tin, and so on; organizations representing specific ideologies (the Organisation for Economic Co-operation and Development (OECD) is widely seen as sponsoring a form of capitalist ideology; Islamic countries formed the Organization of Islamic Cooperation (OIC), earlier known as Organization of the Islamic Conference); and even, if the definition of organizations is broadened, organization for specific projects. There is, for example, a group of states and other entities working together against piracy in Somalia's vicinity, in the form of the Contact Group on Piracy off the Coast of Somalia.

Indeed, the variety is so great that in some sense it is difficult to discern a "law of international organizations".[8] In many respects, each organization has its own rules, and the rules of the UN differ substantively from those of the EU, and of OPEC, and of ASEAN. To the extent that international organizations operate in the world around them, moreover, they are subject to general international law rather than a specific law of international organizations. Nonetheless, even if a law of international organizations cannot be said to exist in a meaningful and coherent manner, it is still useful to discuss international law as it relates to international organizations: international organizations are amongst the main institutions of global governance, and given their importance, they need to be studied in terms both of what they share and in terms of where they and their activities are different from one another.[9] The latter can take place in studies of individual

---

8 See Jan Klabbers, "The Paradox of International Institutional Law", (2008) 5 *International Organizations Law Review* 151–73.

9 Additionally, much international law is produced by or within international organizations, so much so that a recent German text can plausibly treat international law as "institutionalized". See Matthias Ruffert and Christian Walter, *Institutionalisiertes Völkerrecht* (2009).

organizations or groups of organizations;[10] the former will take place in books such as this one.

1.2   Defining international organizations

There are wildly diverging estimates about the number of international organizations existing at any given time. Some put it relatively low, at 250 or thereabouts,[11] whereas others feel they number at least around 350, and probably even more. This signifies a huge intellectual problem at the heart of the discipline: important as international organizations are, there is little agreement on what actually constitutes an international organization. Indeed, of all the entities mentioned above in the opening paragraph of this chapter, only about half qualify indisputably as independent international organizations (UN, WHO, WTO, IMF). UNEP and UNHCR are programmes set up by the UN, and thus not fully independent; the WFP is a joint programme set up by the UN and the FAO, whereas the Basel Committee is part of the Bank for International Settlements (BIS).

Most definitions emphasize that international organizations are usually created between states, on the basis of a treaty, possess at least one organ, and have a will that is distinct from that of its member states ("*volonté distincte*"). According to this definition, well-known entities such as the UN, the WHO, the IMF, or the WTO are all deemed to qualify, as do organizations such as the EU. Equally clearly, this definition, insecure as it is, excludes entities set up by private persons under domestic law, such as the Red Cross, Amnesty International or Greenpeace, as well as businesses such as Microsoft or Unilever.

---

10 The UN and EU in particular have often been subjected to treatment in books. On the UN, see for example, the classic by H.G. Nicholas, *The United Nations as a Political Institution* (3rd edn., 1967) or the more lawyerly study by Robert Kolb, *An Introduction to the Law of the United Nations* (2010). On the EU, the best general overview is Paul Craig and Gráinne de Búrca, *EU Law: Text, Cases and Materials* (5th edn., 2011). An excellent study of the work (rather than the law) of the financial institutions is Ngaire Woods, *The Globalizers: The IMF, the World Bank, and Their Borrowers* (2006), while a fine legal analysis of the WTO is Mary E. Footer, *An Institutional and Normative Analysis of the World Trade Organization* (2006).

11 See Anne Peters and Simone Peter, "International Organizations: Between Technocracy and Democracy", in Bardo Fassbender and Anne Peters (eds.), *The Oxford Handbook of the History of International Law* (2012), 170–97.

Yet, these elements function more like guidelines than hard and fast rules. Most organizations tend to be created between states, but there are exceptions: the WTO counts an international organization (the EU) as one of its founding members, and the EU is a member of several other organizations as well, including the FAO. There is, moreover, at least one organization that was exclusively created by other organizations: the Joint Vienna Institute, set up in the mid-1990s by a number of financial institutions (including the World Bank and the European Bank for Reconstruction and Development (EBRD)) to help eastern European economies with the transition to capitalist market economies. Indeed, often enough these days international organizations enter into partnerships with one another, setting up new entities which may or may not themselves have the status of international organization – or grow into that status. Possible examples include the WFP, the Codex Alimentarius Commission, and UNAIDS. While it is fair to say that neither of these is at the moment generally considered an organization in its own right, all three enjoy a considerable amount of autonomy.[12]

Likewise, whereas organizations are usually set up by means of a treaty, there are exceptions. The Organization for Security and Cooperation in Europe (OSCE) ultimately derives from what many hold to be a merely politically binding agreement, the 1975 Helsinki Final Act. The theory underlying this position is sketchy at best, but the position is nonetheless widely shared. Other entities start life on the basis of a resolution of another organization (typically the UN), and grow into an independent status. This applies to, for example, the United Nations Children's Fund (UNICEF) and the UN Industrial Development Organization (UNIDO). The Nordic Council was created by simultaneous resolutions adopted by the parliaments of the five participating states.

Typically, most international organizations will not have merely one, but several different organs. There is typically a plenary body in which all member states are represented; an executive body to take care of the day-to-day business, and a secretariat to help prepare the regular meetings, take care of translations, and related tasks. Yet, as we will see, the dividing line between an organization having one organ and

---

12 Note also that the late nineteenth-century administrative unions used to accept as members entities that were not independent sovereign states: see Douglas Howland, "An Alternative Mode of International Order: The International Administrative Union in the Nineteenth Century", (2015) 41 *Review of International Studies* 161–83.

a treaty body that is not considered an international organization is a fine one indeed.

The most difficult requirement to apply is that of the distinct will, as this displays a tension between sociological accuracy and legal formalism. In a sociological sense, well-nigh all organizations have a distinct will. As any student of bureaucracy will realize, bureaucracies tend to lead a life of their own; thus, the very idea of a secretariat proposing that an item be placed on the political agenda already suggests that the organization does more than merely faithfully execute the common will of the member states, and thus can be deemed to have a distinct will. Yet, from a formalist angle, the distinct will may not be all that obvious. There are, after all, precious few organizations that can take binding decisions against the will of one or more member states; the EU is in a position to do this, as is the UN (or rather its Security Council), but there are few additional examples available. From such an angle then, few organizations actually possess a distinct will. The drawback then is that inevitably, without such a distinct will, organizations will be seen as vehicles for their member states and nothing more, and that seems sociologically inaccurate.

So if there is some certainty at the core, there is enormous uncertainty at the penumbra. Sometimes, for example, international tribunals are treated as international organizations, and indeed they do tick all boxes: international courts are typically created by states, on the basis of a treaty, with at least one organ (in other words, the court itself), and a will distinct from that of its member states – after all, judicial independence demands nothing less. And yet, upon closer scrutiny there is something awkward about treating international courts as international organizations. It is sometimes held, for example, that organizations exercise delegated powers, yet to think of courts as exercising delegated powers is awkward, if only because it suggests that the member states can interfere with judicial independence. It is also unclear whether so-called treaty-bodies should be seen as international organizations, in particular if their set up is so informal as to suggest that their founding fathers were not all that keen on creating rigid institutions. This consideration applies perhaps most prominently to the various Committees of the Parties, and Meetings of the Parties, set up under multilateral agreements to protect the environment. These are envisaged as loose, flexible structures – rather the opposite of the big and entrenched bureaucracies that international organizations are sometimes thought to be.

There is further uncertainty regarding military alliances such as NATO or, in the southern hemisphere, ANZUS (this stands for Australia, New Zealand, United States Security Treaty). These tend to meet the criteria mentioned above, at least if some decision-making body is envisaged (as is often the case) and yet, their status as international organizations is uncertain.[13] This finds its cause partly in the often fleeting nature of military alliances: today's enemy may be tomorrow's friend, and the other way around, so alliances are traditionally deemed to be less than stable, let alone permanent. Additionally, they may often be dominated by a single member state to such an extent (think USSR with respect to Warsaw Pact, or the US with respect to both NATO and ANZUS) that some hold that in such cases, the organization is but a vehicle for that dominant member state, and thus not really manifesting an entity with a will of its own. This argument has a long pedigree: it was already mentioned by Frank Sayre in 1919, discussing the dominance of the Suez Commission by the United Kingdom (UK).[14]

Some entities, finally, are little more than interest groups, defending and promoting the interests of their member states. The most obvious example is, in all likelihood, OPEC, but on a different level, the same basic thought may apply to most regional organizations, including the EU. While these entities typically refer to some notion of the public good in their constituent documents, they equally typically also carve out some special position for their own region and their own member states. And some of these entities compete, on open markets, with private institutions: this applies, for example, to the European University Institute (EUI), set up as an international organization and competing with regular universities for available staff and students as well as research funding. The BIS, moreover, used to have private shareholders: some of these started arbitration proceedings against the organization when they were being bought out against, they felt, too little compensation.[15]

All this can lead to serious practical legal issues. OPEC, for example, has been on the receiving end of anti-trust investigations in the US, whereas the Court of Justice of the European Union (CJEU) had

---

13 This applies in particular to ANZUS, which embodies a looser form of cooperation than NATO and, symbolically perhaps, lacks the word "organization" in its name.

14 See Sayre, *Experiments*, 77.

15 See *Reineccius and others* v. *Bank for International Settlements*, Permanent Court of Arbitration, partial award of 22 November 2002.

to address the question whether Eurocontrol, tasked with air control issues in Europe, was best seen as a commercial "undertaking" within the meaning of EU law. Yet, ever since the publication of Sayre's *Experiments in International Administration* almost a century ago, the law of international organizations tends to adopt a broad approach to what constitutes an international organization and, what is more, tends to treat all organizations alike.[16] Most organizations can benefit from immunity from suit and taxation, regardless of the sort of work they do and whose interests they serve.

1.3   Legal dynamics

International organizations are puzzling creatures, and have long created serious analytical problems for international lawyers. On the one hand, these stem from what may be called their "layered" nature: international organizations are created by states and perform functions delegated to them by states, but they do not replace states. The member states remain visible, and it is often the case that there is a temptation to reduce the acts of the organization to an act of all or some of its member states.[17]

Perhaps an example may clarify the point. Suppose Taiwan, currently not generally recognized as an independent state, were to apply for admission to the UN. This can only be realized if the Security Council recommends Taiwan for admission, and in the Security Council, China has a possibility to veto Taiwan's application. Should China indeed exercise its veto, how then is the decision to reject Taiwan's application to be regarded? From one angle it is a decision by the Security Council, taken in accordance with the UN Charter. From a different angle the decision is one by China, reluctant to admit Taiwan as accepting Taiwan could be seen as recognition of its sovereignty. In 2011 the International Court of Justice (ICJ) was confronted with a similar setting, when the Former Yugoslav Republic of Macedonia (FYROM) complained that Greece had blocked its admission to NATO and had therewith violated its obligation towards FYROM under a bilateral agreement. Precisely because FYROM brought the case in this manner,

---

16 See generally Jan Klabbers, "Unity, Diversity, Accountability: The Ambivalent Concept of International Organisation", (2013) 14 *Melbourne Journal of International Law* 149–70.

17 The most sophisticated conceptual study is Catherine M. Brölmann, *The Institutional Veil in Public International Law: International Organisations and the Law of Treaties* (2007).

the Court could afford to see Greece's behaviour as, indeed, the behaviour of Greece under a bilateral agreement; it did not need to analyse the extent to which NATO qua organization had been involved and, as a result, the ICJ did little to clarify the relationship between states and their organizations.[18]

If partly the uncertainty concerning international organizations stems from their layered nature, with states always remaining visible behind the organization, partly it also stems from the limits of functionalism. Functionalism, by far the dominant theory concerning the law of international organizations, is in essence a theory precisely about the relations between organizations and their member states.[19] It is essentially a form of principal–agent theory: member states (the principal) delegate tasks to an agent, typically one they have created for the purpose. Still, there are a few peculiar characteristics. One is that the principal here is invariably a collective principal: a single state on its own cannot establish an international organization. Additionally, there is the peculiarity that the principal is represented within the agent: all organizations will have a plenary organ in which the member states are represented.

In its focus on relations between the organization and its member states, functionalism has considerable explanatory force. It can help explain why organizations have certain powers (competences) but not others; it can help explain the fact that well-nigh all international organizations enjoy privileges and immunities (from prosecution, from taxation, and so on); it can help explain why and how organizations can limit access and reject aspiring member states or suspend or expel members; and it can help explain why some organizations have law-making prerogatives whereas others do not. But the essential point is that functionalism, being devised to say something about the relations between organizations and their members, cannot say anything about topics where this relationship is not at issue.[20]

---

18 See *Application of the Interim Accord of 13 September 1995* (*Former Yugoslav Republic of Macedonia v. Greece*), [2011] ICJ Reports 644.

19 See Michel Virally, "La notion de fonction dans la théorie de l'organisation internationale", in Suzanne Bastid et al. (eds.), *Mélanges offerts à Charles Rousseau: La communauté international* (1974), 277–300; Niels M. Blokker, "International Organizations and their Members", (2004) 1 *International Organizations Law Review* 139–61.

20 See generally Jan Klabbers, "Theorising International Organisations", in Florian Hoffmann and Anne Orford (eds.), *The Oxford Handbook of International Legal Theory* (forthcoming).

There are, broadly, two groups of topics that fall outside the purview of functionalism. Functionalism has very little to say about things that go on inside the organization. Thus, relations between the organization and its employees have traditionally been left outside the scope of functionalism, precisely because these do not involve the member states. The relationship between the UN and its current Secretary-General Ban Ki-moon is a relationship between an organization and an individual. While it is plausible that he owes his appointment in part to his nationality (the post is habitually filled by a form of rotation amongst continents, and South Korea is not a state surrounded by a great deal of political controversy), nonetheless the relationship is not between the UN and South Korea, but between the UN and Ban Ki-moon. And what applies to him, applies across the board. The legal counsel of the WHO may happen to be an Italian citizen at present, but the relevant relationship is between the individual and the WHO, not his state of nationality.

Much the same applies to relations between organs of international organizations. Here, too, the member states hardly enter the picture, except to the extent that they themselves act as organs. And where the member states are relevant, the relevance of their relations with other organs becomes transformed into something less member state focused: the relations between the plenary body and the executive body of an organization are typically cast in terms not of functionalism, but in terms of public law concepts borrowed from domestic settings – institutional balance, or checks and balances. The member states together may form the plenary, but relations between plenary and others become abstracted from those member states or, put differently, the member states and the plenary are simultaneously both identical (the same states, after all) and radically different.

The second larger topic or group of topics that falls outside the purview of functionalism concerns relations between the organization and the outside world.[21] Since functionalism is limited to discussing issues between the organization and its own member states, it has little to say about things that do not (or not only) involve those member states but affect a wider group of persons or actors. As long as organizations

---

21 Note how this division into three legal dynamics also informs the structure of this book. Chapters 2, 3 and 4 are devoted to the relations between the organization and its members; chapter 5 addresses internal affairs, while chapters 6 and 7 discuss various aspects of the organization's external relations.

had a largely internal focus (the organization taking care of things for its member states and mostly affecting those states qua states rather than their citizens[22]) this did not create many problems, but as soon as organizations went out in the world the problems became visible. Thus, while organizations may derive their treaty-making powers from their member states, they cannot invoke functionalist thought in their treaty relations with third parties. If there is a treaty between the EU and Japan, Japan might be forgiven for thinking that such a treaty need not be interpreted in light of the EU's functional concerns – why not, after all, apply it in light of Japan's concerns? This even applies to treaties involving the organization's own member states, such as headquarters agreements. The ICJ had great difficulties, in 1980, in deciding on how the headquarters agreement between the WHO and Egypt could be terminated, and the problem stemmed precisely from the circumstance that Egypt was not just a member state, but played a double role: it was also the WHO's treaty partner, since it hosted one of the WHO's regional offices. As a result, the WHO could not simply decide to terminate the agreement, for doing so would inevitably affect Egypt, the treaty partner.[23]

More conspicuously still, functionalism runs into problems with respect to the possible responsibility of international organizations. When organizations start to administer territory and thus start to take on governmental tasks, their acts come to affect directly and immediately the daily lives of the people within their jurisdiction. The most well-known examples are formed by the UN's governance of East Timor and Kosovo around the turn of the century. In such circumstances, the organization can negatively affect people's lives, and can do wrong. Likewise, when UNHCR runs a refugee camp or handles refugee applications, any decision it takes may come to affect individuals. When the World Bank sponsors a development project which causes many people to be displaced, individual lives are affected, and the same applies when the International Organization for Migration (IOM) runs immigration processing centres on behalf of states. In those circumstances, functionalism offers little help: as a theory on

---

22 The statement as such is theoretically highly problematic: even if organizations mostly address states qua states, nonetheless their activities will have a profound impact on the citizens of those states. For illuminating discussion, see Guy F. Sinclair, "State Formation, Liberal Reform, and the Growth of International Organizations", available at http://papers.ssrn.com/sol3/papers. cfm?abstract_id=2545767 (visited 23 January 2015).

23 See *Interpretation of the Agreement of 25 March 1951 between the WHO and Egypt*, advisory opinion, [1980] ICJ Reports73. The case is discussed in more detail in Chapter 6 below.

relations between states and organizations, it does not, and cannot, accommodate individuals. Solving a mishandled refugee application by invoking functionalism will inevitably result in a finding that the organization could not have done wrong: it did what it did in the exercise of its functions, so how could this be wrong? And yet, the refugee in question may be sent back to a certain death after a mishandled application; thousands of people may remain in limbo after being displaced during a World Bank project. In such a setting, where the position of third parties is at stake, functionalism simply has no traction, and it is this circumstance which helps explain why the responsibility of international organizations has become such a vexing topic.

2 The legal existence of international organizations

2.1 Introduction

When international organizations were first created, their legal status remained uncertain. The early organizations of the nineteenth century were often hosted by the government of their host state (meaning that the organization was located in an office within a local ministry), and were often predominantly staffed by citizens of their host state and typically paid for by the host government, with the member states merely financing the travel back and forth of their representatives. In these circumstances, little thought was given to issues of legal status or personality.

This situation lasted, curiously enough perhaps, until after the Second World War. The treaties establishing earlier organizations such as the League of Nations did not contain anything on issues of status or personality: the closest the League Covenant came was to grant diplomatic status to its officials and to representatives of its member states and proclaim the inviolability of the League's premises, in article 7.

Still, it was quickly realized that if the organization was to act effectively, it would have to insulate itself against the host state, for instance by hiring people from abroad. To this end, an international civil service mentality needed to be created,[24] and it became necessary to allow the organization to act within the domestic legal order of the host state and, quite possibly, other states as well. But how to achieve this? After all, while domestic legal orders typically recognize a variety of legal persons (the association, the foundation, the partnership, the limited liability company), few domestic legal orders will specify anything about international organizations as legal persons, and even if they would, the risk is that the domestic legal order concerned insists on characteristics that might be considered undesirable to other member

---

24 See Chapter 5 section 5.4 below.

states. Thus, if Swiss law were to say that organizations can act under Swiss law provided they have a certain minimum situation of financial stability, others might see this as extortion.

Hence, the only viable solution, so it seemed, was to provide for domestic legal personality in the constituent document. This way, all member states could have a say in the precise scope of personality, and the host state could not get away with imposing burdens on the other member states. As a result, many organizational constitutions provide at the very least that the organization has in the domestic legal orders of its member states "such legal capacity as may be necessary for the exercise of its functions",[25] and often further specify that the legal capacity under domestic law encompasses at least the capacity to contract, to acquire and dispose of movable and immovable property, and to institute legal proceedings. Hence, organizations can conclude labour contracts with their staff and contracts for services, can own property, and can go to court if they so desire.

There is one obvious limit here: the constituent document of an organization can, at best, only provide that the organization has domestic personality in its own member states; due to the classic *pacta tertiis* maxim,[26] it cannot grant legal personality elsewhere. In other words: whether the EU can act under Brazilian law depends not on the EU treaty (Brazil, after all, is not a member of the EU), but on Brazilian law. Likewise, whether the OAS can act in non-member state Belgium depends on Belgium, not on the OAS constitution.[27]

2.2   International legal personality

While the standard definition of international organizations does not insist on organizations possessing international legal personality, there is a strong feeling that organizations somehow need to possess such personality in order to be able to act under international law. Thus, the articles on the responsibility of international organizations, adopted

---

25 The words are taken from article 104 of the UN Charter.

26 Treaties can create neither rights nor obligations for third parties without their consent. The maxim is codified in articles 34–36 of the VCLT. The seminal study is Christine Chinkin, *Third Parties in International Law* (1993).

27 Local courts can be creative in allowing organizations to act: see for example, in the UK the classic case of *Arab Monetary Fund* v. *Hashim and others*, House of Lords, 21 February 1991, reproduced in 85 ILR 1.

by the International Law Commission (ILC) in 2011, apply only to organizations possessing international legal personality: entities lacking personality cannot be held responsible, and this suggests rather strongly that entities devoid of personality are not proper international organizations at all.

This is curious, largely for two reasons. The first reason is that very few organizations are explicitly granted international legal personality. The main exception, until the 1990s, was formed by the financial institutions: the constitutions of entities such as the IMF and the World Bank were amongst the few constitutions that contained a specific clause granting them international legal personality. The reason for this was obvious: where there is a lot of money at stake, the member states must be shielded against possible claims for wrongdoings by their organization. Consequently, it was thought that if the organization possessed separate legal personality, its member states could not be held responsible for financial debts of the organization or other financial troubles.

By contrast, however, many organizations lacked a specific grant of international legal personality. The Treaty establishing the European Economic Community (EEC, now EU) merely provided, in the pithiest of phrases, that the EU "shall have legal personality", leaving unanswered the question whether this personality referred to domestic law, or to international law.[28] And the UN Charter contained nothing on the topic, largely because the drafters held that a specific clause would be unnecessary at any rate: to their mind, an actor cannot itself decide on its own legal status – instead, this is a matter for the legal system concerned to decide. In other words, they felt that the legal personality of the UN under international law would depend on international law rather than on the intentions of the parties. Merely proclaiming "we hereby create an international legal person" would not do the trick unless the legal system (international law) would accept such a statement as decisive.

The question of the international legal personality of international organizations came before the ICJ in 1949, in *Reparation for Injuries*,[29] but did so in a curious manner. Just a little while after the UN had

---

28   The CJEU would find it to refer to personality under international law, but without providing an explanation. See Case 22/70, *Commission v. Council* [1971] ECR 273.

29   See *Reparation for Injuries Suffered in the Service of the United Nations*, advisory opinion, [1949] ICJ Reports 174.

been established, large unrest broke out in the Middle East when plans were made to create the state of Israel. The UN sent a mediating mission headed by a Swedish nobleman, Count Folke Bernadotte. Count Bernadotte lost his life in an attack attributed to a group of Zionist activists and the question arose who would have to pay for hospital costs, the costs of shipping corpses back to Europe, and so on. The UN contemplated bringing a claim for compensation against Israel, but faced two legal problems. First, the UN Charter did not give it any specific competence to bring claims, second, Israel was, at the relevant time, not a member state of the UN.

It was this second question that the Court addressed first, and it did so in the form of a discussion on international legal personality. The underlying theory seemed to be that if the UN were found to possess international legal personality, then Israel could not claim that it could legally ignore the existence of the UN.

The Court would indeed find that the UN possessed international legal personality, but it remains somewhat unclear on what basis it reached its finding.[30] It seemed to derive the personality of the UN mostly from its activities. The UN, so the Court remarked, is engaged in a set of activities which can only be explained on the basis of the organization possessing international legal personality. The Court suggested that the UN had been positioned against its own member states through such notions as its domestic legal capacity and the grant of privileges and immunities, and that the UN was empowered to conclude international agreements. Practice then, so the Court continued, confirmed this separate character of the UN, separate from its member states, and some conventions, such as the 1946 Convention on Privileges and Immunities, only bolstered this conclusion: "It is difficult to see how such a convention could operate except upon the international plane and as between parties possessing international personality".[31]

The example was, in fact, badly chosen:[32] the UN was not, and still is not, a party to the 1946 Convention – at best it can be seen as a beneficiary. Hence, to use the 1946 Convention in order to demonstrate

---

30 It is for this reason that the opinion has been invoked in support of diametrically opposed theories concerning international legal personality.

31 See *Reparation*, 179.

32 This was not the Court's finest moment at any rate: elsewhere it refers to a precedent that does not at all say what the Court claims it said. See *Reparation*, 182–3.

the separate legal personality of the UN misses the point by a considerable margin. The wider point, however, was developed with some sophistication: the international legal personality of organizations can be demonstrated with the help of their practices. If they engage in international activities, then international legal personality may well be presumed: ". . . the Organization was intended to exercise and enjoy, and is in fact exercising and enjoying, functions and rights which can only be explained on the basis of the possession of a large measure of international personality. . .".[33]

This laid the foundation for finding that the UN possessed international legal personality, but the Court needed to go one step further still in order to dismiss the possible argument by Israel that whatever the position of the UN vis-à-vis its own members would be, it could not be opposable to non-members such as (at the time) Israel. Hence, the Court had to say something about the personality not merely being inter-subjectively valid between the member states, but having an objective validity. Here, the Court eventually held that the power of numbers was considerable: ". . . fifty states, representing the vast majority of the members of the international community, had the power, in conformity with international law, to bring into being an entity possessing objective international personality, and not merely personality recognized by them alone . . .".[34]

While the *Reparation* opinion helped to solve the crisis that inspired its request, on the point of personality it raised more questions than it answered. It provided ammunition for what became the most popular theory on personality, the so-called "will theory". The "will theory" holds that eventually the will of the drafters is decisive. If the drafters grant personality, then the organization will have such personality. Conversely, if the drafters withhold personality, then the organization will be devoid of personality. This theory is popular largely because it places states in the driving seat, but has little to recommend it. For one thing, it faces empirical problems of considerable magnitude, since very few constitutional documents provide explicitly for international legal personality. Surely, it cannot be maintained that the International Labour Organization (ILO) is not a legal person because its constitution does not refer to personality, or that the IMO is not a legal person for purposes of international law because its constitution lacks a clause to this effect.

---

33 See *Reparation*, 179.
34 See *Reparation*, 185.

Sometimes this is recognized, and the position somewhat softened: an organization with international tasks will have personality due to the founders' will, because the founders have given it those international tasks. Others, starting from a related mindset, would hold that what matters is recognition: if the organization has contacts with third parties, those others recognize it, and thus it has legal personality. But this not only places the cart in front of the horse, it is also inconsistent: if recognition by third parties is decisive, then by definition it is not the will of the founders that is decisive.

This messy theoretical situation prompted Norwegian international lawyer Finn Seyersted to formulate a radically different theory: the theory of "objective personality".[35] For Seyersted, each and every organization would possess international legal personality, provided it would meet the threshold of "organizationhood": if an entity is an organization, then it is also an international legal person, in much the same way as a state, once its statehood is established, is an international person.[36] This theory has the great benefit of not having to rely on the subjective and often silent intentions of founders,[37] but the considerable disadvantage of uncertainty. After all, as noted earlier, there simply is no generally accepted definition of "international organization", and therefore also no generally recognized threshold for "organizationhood". In addition, Seyersted's theory quickly assumes a *jus cogens* character: if the founders actively want their organization to have no legal personality at all (admittedly a rather hypothetical position), then how can Seyersted justify that such an organization has personality despite the explicit intentions of the drafters? If the "will theory" overestimates the intentions of the drafters, Seyersted's "objective theory" underestimates them.

---

35 Not to be confused with the theory relating to the objective validity of organizations as endorsed by the ICJ in *Reparation*, although it is fair to say that an organization with Seyerstedian objective personality would automatically be objectively valid.

36 See Finn Seyersted, *Objective International Personality of Intergovernmental Organizations: Do their Capacities Really Depend on the Conventions Establishing Them?* (1963). A synthesis of much of his work was posthumously published as Finn Seyersted, *Common Law of International Organizations* (2008).

37 The EU for example, when first established in the early 1990s on top of the existing EC, had not been endowed with international legal personality. Many concluded that therefore it lacked such personality, despite the EU having a foreign policy and an immigration policy – tasks that demand international action by definition. For discussion, see Jan Klabbers, "Presumptive Personality: The European Union in International Law", in Martti Koskenniemi (ed.), *International Law Aspects of the European Union* (1998), 231–53.

In recent decades, a third theory has been proposed which aims to find a middle ground under the heading of presumptive personality.[38] Here the basic idea is that organizations (including entities of uncertain "organizationhood") are presumed to possess international legal personality until the opposite can be demonstrated, for example if the constitution contains an explicit clause denying personality, or if the organization has no external relations and lacks the competences to engage in such relations. As a result, most organizations will be seen to possess personality, and this, it is felt, accurately reflects the practice whereby organizations engage in all sorts of activities that, as *Reparation* proposed, can only be explained on the basis of some measure of personality. The presumptive theory therewith does justice to objective criteria (as does Seyersted), but keeps the door open for the member states to decide differently (as does the "will theory").

2.3   Powers

In the early days of international organizations, few observers saw fit to treat them as institutions and pay attention to their institutional qualities. Instead, for many, the treaties creating international organizations were seen as, simply, treaties, and even the Permanent Court of International Justice (PCIJ) saw fit to regard early requests for advisory opinions on the permissible range of activities of the ILO as simply questions relating to interpretation of the ILO constitution.[39]

By the mid-1920s however, the PCIJ realized that there was something going on which could not be grasped by a simple treaty paradigm.[40] In 1927, confronted with a question about the scope of the jurisdiction of the European Danube Commission, it developed instead an institutional notion: the European Danube Commission was given certain functions, and had been granted certain powers to give effect to those functions. In other words, instead of treating the activities of organizations as a matter of treaty interpretation pure and simple, the Court had now formulated a theory of attributed or conferred powers:

---

38 See Jan Klabbers, "Presumptive Personality". The theory is embedded in a larger theoretical framework in Jan Klabbers, "Lawmaking and Constitutionalism", in Jan Klabbers, Anne Peters and Geir Ulfstein, *The Constitutionalization of International Law* (2009), 81–125.

39 See generally Jan Klabbers, "The Life and Times of the Law of International Orgnizations", (2001) 70 *Nordic Journal of International Law* 287–317.

40 See generally Viljam Engström, *Constructing the Powers of International Institutions* (2012).

organizations have the powers (competences) their members endow them with.[41]

This nicely settled the case before it, but the one major problem with such a conception became visible very rapidly: what to do if a situation arises which the member states never considered? A strict reading of the attributed powers doctrine would suggest that in such a case, the organization simply could not act for want of a legal power to do so, but this, so it was intuitively realized, may be difficult to reconcile with the very functioning of the organization: what if it could be argued that the organization would need a certain power in order to properly execute its tasks, but the members had never considered the scenario?

In such a case, so the same PCIJ decided a year or so later, the organization can imply certain powers from the existence of those explicitly attributed powers. Colloquially put, a power to walk the dog implies the power first to put the dog on its leash, as otherwise the expressly granted power (to walk the dog) cannot be given effect. In the case actually before the Court, an agreement between Turkey and Greece had created a Mixed Commission to oversee implementation of the agreement. In some cases, moreover, if the Mixed Commission could not decide, resort could be had to arbitration, but the agreement failed to specify which party or parties could instigate arbitration proceedings. Here, then, the Court had little problem in finding that such power had by implication been granted to the Mixed Commission itself: its power to decide included the power to resort to arbitration if necessary, even if the latter had not been spelled out.[42]

This already gave organizations quite a bit of leeway: a desire to act on a certain topic could often be justified by reference to such action being required to give effect to other powers. But after the Second World War the ICJ would take things considerably further still. In the above-mentioned *Reparation* case, it launched the idea that organizations can utilize powers that are implied not just in the existence of express powers, but are needed in light of the organization's very existence. It may be recalled that the main question before the Court was whether the UN would possess the power to bring a claim against Israel. The UN

---

41 See *Jurisdiction of the European Commission of the Danube between Galatz and Braila*, advisory opinion, [1927] Series B, no. 14, at 64.

42 See *Interpretation of the Greco–Turkish Agreement of December 1st, 1926*, advisory opinion, [1928] Publ. PCIJ, Series B, no. 16, at 20.

Charter was silent on the matter, so no power to this effect had been actively attributed to the UN. Nonetheless, so the Court famously held, under international law "the Organization must be deemed to have those powers which, though not expressly provided in the Charter, are conferred upon it by necessary implication as being essential to the performance of its duties".[43]

There are two relevant points to note. First, the Court unashamedly broadened the basis of implication. In the 1928 *Greco-Turkish* opinion, what was still required was a connection to an express power; in *Reparation*, decided two decades later, the Court gave up its insistence on such a connection, and proved happy to accept a mere link to the organization's general duties.[44] Needless to say, this made it much easier for the organization to justify activities that have little or no basis in the original constitution, and equally needless to say, it was exactly this broad version of the doctrine that would become hugely popular. The broad approach to the implied powers doctrine was confirmed by the ICJ in later opinions,[45] and would allow organizations to expand their activities beyond recognition.[46]

The second point to note is somewhat more complicated. It is a general proposition in international law that rules of law can generally only be made on the basis of state consent, and that states cannot, normally speaking, become legally bound without having expressed their consent to become legally bound. In this light, the implied powers doctrine might be vulnerable to critique: after all, it suggests that organizations can engage in all sorts of activities regardless of state consent, and perhaps even in opposition to the interests of some or all of the organization's member states. Hence, it would be strategically and rhetorically useful if somehow the implied powers doctrine and state consent could be aligned, and the Court did precisely this when it stipulated that implied powers arose "by necessary

---

43 See *Reparation*, 182.

44 As a result, Seyersted argued that effectively the law had accepted a doctrine not of implied powers, but of inherent powers – organizations can do as they please (in the same way as states) within the limits of international law and as long as activities are not prohibited in their constitutions. See Seyersted, *Common Law*.

45 Most notably perhaps in *Effect of Awards of Compensation Made by the United Nations Administrative Tribunal*, [1954] ICJ Reports 47, and *Certain Expenses of the United Nations (Article 17, Paragraph 2, of the Charter)*, [1962] ICJ Reports 151.

46 The CJEU embraced a slightly different version, geared at protecting the unity of EU law, in Case 22/70.

implication". The point was not solely to say that organizations can pick and choose – no, the point was to make clear that implied powers were implied "by necessary implication"; they followed, in other words, from the very edifice that the member states had created, and thus could be traced back to and aligned with the intentions and consent of the member states. The Court used the even stronger phrase "by necessary intendment" in later cases, suggesting that, if anything, implied powers were firmly rooted in the intentions of the drafters.

What the Court did not yet realize in the late 1940s, but what became clear later on, is that the organization's expanded scope of powers comes at a price: the price of control. Organizations such as the UN engage in many, many activities that can only be traced back with some difficulty to the UN Charter. The UN occupies itself with a myriad of activities, ranging from the fight against HIV/Aids to drugs trafficking and crime prevention, and ranging from human settlement to climate change. Admittedly, the UN's mandate is cast in broad terms to begin with but, even so, not all of its activities can with great plausibility be cast in terms of its general function and purposes. The result is that the UN can be, and sometimes is, accused of "running wild": there is but a thin line between a responsible use of the implied powers doctrine and what in military circles is referred to as "mission creep". And what applies to the UN applies to most organizations: the emergence and popularity of the implied powers doctrine has resulted in organizations expanding the scope of their activities so much that member states felt they had to regain control.

It is no coincidence that during the 1990s the climate changed.[47] In particular, the EU member states made a point of carving the principle of attributed powers in stone, and inserted the notion of subsidiarity in EU law. According to the subsidiarity principle, political decision-making should take place at the most appropriate level. And while there is a lot about the principle that is unclear,[48] the fact that the EU member states felt the need to explicitly lay down the doctrine of attribution and insert the principle of subsidiarity can only be interpreted as a sign to the EU that expansion of the scope of activities had reached the limits

---

47   See Jan Klabbers, "The Changing Image of International Organizations", in Jean-Marc Coicaud and Veijo Heiskanen (eds.), *The Legitimacy of International Organizations* (2001), 221–55.

48   A particularly vigorous critique is Gareth Davies, "Subsidiarity: The Wrong Idea, In the Wrong Place, At the Wrong Time", (2006) 43 *Common Market Law Review* 63–84.

of acceptability.[49] In like manner, the CJEU stopped rubberstamping the EU's ever-growing reach, even if its motives may not always have been equally pure. In *Opinion 2/94*, rendered in 1996, it held that the EU lacked the power to accede to the European Convention on Human Rights (ECHR),[50] and in *Opinion 1/94*, it held that in matters of international trade, an implied power needed not merely to be linked to the EU's goals, but needed to be "inextricably linked", and found *in casu* that such a strong link did not exist.[51]

In other organizations no such constitutional amendments took place, but even there the writing was often on the wall. In the UN, for example, one very prominent member state spent much of the 1980s and 1990s teasing the UN by threatening to withhold funds unless the organization would tone down its activities – never mind that membership contributions are compulsory. Other organizations went through similar financial crises, often brought about by dissatisfaction with the broad range of activities of the organization – and sometimes at the expense of what had originally been conceived as the organization's core task.

2.4   Constitutions

International organizations are, almost invariably, set up on the basis of a treaty, and this provokes the question whether there is something special about the treaties establishing institutions, so much so that such treaties should be given preferential treatment.[52] It is, for instance, often suggested that the constituent documents of international organizations should be interpreted in broad, teleological fashion, and this follows more or less directly from functionalist thought. Organizations, under functionalism, are set up to perform

---

49 With the 2009 Lisbon amendments, moreover, the EU member states more or less formally abolished the implied powers doctrine: articles 4(1) and 5(2) TEU emphasize that competences not explicitly conferred on the EU remain with the member states.

50 See *Opinion 2/94 (European Convention on Human Rights)* [1996] ECR I-1759. Here one may wonder about the purity of the Court's motives, in that the CJEU would at any rate be reluctant to submit itself to the jurisdiction of the ECtHR. For much the same reason it opined, in December 2014 (*Opinion 2/13*, nyr) that the draft agreement on accession to the European Convention was incompatible with EU law.

51 See *Opinion 1/94 (WTO)* [1994] ECR I-5267.

52 See, for example, Shabtai Rosenne, "Is the Constitutional Instrument of an International Organization an International Treaty?", in Shabtai Rosenne, *Developments in the Law of Treaties 1945–1986* (1989), 181–258.

a function; the function is deemed generally worthwhile; hence, the work of organizations should be facilitated and hence, their constituent documents should be interpreted generously.[53]

General international law seems reluctant to recognize a legally relevant distinction between various kinds of treaties.[54] Some have suggested that human rights treaties are somehow special, and while this is intuitively plausible, it proves difficult to give any legal effect to distinctions between human rights treaties and other treaties.[55] Some observers have pointed out that some constituent documents have rather lofty designations. The document on which the UN is based is a Charter; the League of Nations invoked the biblical term Covenant, and sometimes constituent documents are called Constitutions.[56] It follows, so the argument seems to go, that these documents are best seen as constitutions, suggesting the analogy of a domestic distinction between constitution and legislation: treaties establishing international organizations are thought of as constitutions, whereas other treaties would resemble legislation.

The argument is unconvincing, for at least three reasons. First, it remains unsupported by the Vienna Convention on the Law of Treaties (VCLT) which, in article 2, specifies that treaties have the same legal character irrespective of their designation.[57] Second, it is gainsaid by the designation of some rather relevant organizations: the EU's basic document is, rather mundanely, simply referred to as Treaty on European Union (TEU), while the IMF and World Bank

---

53 Note however that the constitutional documents do no exhaust the matter: they are embedded in a broader framework of agreements. A good example is the informal but strong agreement that the World Bank shall be headed by an American while the IMF shall be under European leadership. For a fine discussion, see Jacob Katz Cogan, "Representation and Power in International Organization: The Operational Constitution and Its Critics", (2009) 103 *American Journal of International Law* 209–63.

54 There is no support for a substantive distinction in the 1969 VCLT. At best, the Vienna Convention allows for distinctions based on number of parties (bilateral versus multilateral); it even has problems accommodating a distinction between contractual and law-making treaties.

55 For intelligent discussion, see Matthew Craven, "Legal Differentiation and the Concept of the Human Rights Treaty in International Law", (2000) 11 *European Journal of International Law* 489–520.

56 Fassbender makes the point with respect to the UN, suggesting rightly that the term Charter denotes an "especially elevated class" of instrument, but holding rather optimistically that "there is no doubt that in 1945 the term 'charter' was understood to be equivalent to 'written constitution'". See Bardo Fassbender, *The United Nations Charter as the Constitution of the International Community* (2009), at 88 and 89, respectively.

57 See generally Jan Klabbers, *The Concept of Treaty in International Law* (1996).

are based on "Articles of Agreement" – not a very lofty designation either. Yet, if anything, the EU is arguably the most "constitutional" of international organizations, with its parliament and court and the direct effect and supremacy of its rules.[58] And third, outside the EU context,[59] the scarce case-law that can be considered relevant does not support any privileged position for the treaties establishing international organizations.

A case in point is the advisory opinion of the ICJ on the setting up of the Maritime Safety Committee of what was at the time still the IMCO.[60] According to the constitution of IMCO, the Maritime Safety Committee would have to include the eight largest ship-owning nations, which raised the question how to identify those: should one look for registered tonnage? In that case, the eight largest included two states with dubious track records on issues of safety: Liberia and Panama offer their services as flag states of convenience. Alternatively, with the goals of IMCO and its Maritime Safety Committee in mind, the decisive criterion could have been (as some states argued) nationality of ownership: in that case, Liberia and Panama could legitimately be excluded. A teleological approach would have favoured the latter interpretation, but the Court followed the former, more literal interpretation, focusing on the text of the relevant provision and eventually holding that normal shipping practice equates ship owning with registration.[61]

While the VCLT does not make a principled distinction between categories of treaties, it occasionally recognizes that the treaties establishing international organizations present specific practical questions. In a general clause, article 5 allows for the rules of the organization to deviate from the Vienna Convention. Thus, organizations may well adopt specific rules on how to interpret their constituent instruments,

---

58 The seminal article is Eric Stein, "Lawyers, Judges, and the Making of a Transnational Constitution", (1981) 75 *American Journal of International Law* 1–27.

59 The CJEU has been very teleological in its interpretation of the EU treaties, especially in early cases such as Case 26/62, *Van Gend & Loos* v. *Nederlandse Administratie der Belastingen* [1963] ECR 1, and Case 6/64, *Flaminio Costa* v. *ENEL* [1964] ECR 585. Note though that the CJEU is a court internal to the organization on whose behalf it works; it has something at stake in stimulating the expansion of the EU.

60 See *Constitution of the Maritime Safety Committee of the Inter-Governmental Maritime Consultative Organization*, advisory opinion, [1960] ICJ Reports 150.

61 The leading monograph is Tetsuo Sato, *Evolving Constitutions of International Organizations* (1996). Note that Sato is much in favour of a teleological approach, but explicitly presents it as aspirational.

or how to terminate them, or whether and in what circumstances reservations are allowed.

The VCLT generally functions as a default treaty: many of its rules are residual in nature, meaning that states may use them but are often also allowed to depart from them if they can think of a solution more suitable for their needs. In the absence of anything specific on reservations to constituent instruments, article 20(3) VCLT holds that matters relating to reservations to organizational instruments shall be decided by the "competent organ", leaving it to the organization and its member states to designate which of the organs shall be deemed competent.[62]

When it comes to amending constituent instruments, organizations will typically have envisaged their own procedures. Often, these involve a two-tier process: a proposed amendment must first be approved by the plenary organ of the organization, and subsequently be approved by the member states individually in accordance with their respective domestic procedures. Sometimes amendments become binding on all member states upon having been accepted by a majority of member states – in such a case, members that disapprove of the amendment face the stark choice of whether to withdraw from the organization, or whether reluctantly to accept the amendment after all. This kind of setting requires intelligent political management: the executive organ is well-advised to only stimulate amendment if it is clear that the amendment will carry large and widespread support.[63]

It is a logical consequence of state sovereignty that amendments will normally involve new obligations for the member states, and it follows that such new obligations must thus be approved by the state's treaty-making authorities. This does entail, however, that amendment can be a cumbersome and protracted process, and it should come as no surprise that, often enough, organizations resort to informal amendment, either by means of authoritative interpretations; by means of an

---

62 Seminal is Maurice Mendelson, "Reservations to the Constitutions of International Organizations", (1971) 45 *British Yearbook of International Law* 137–71.

63 In smaller organizations, amendments may need to be accepted unanimously by all member states, giving each of them an effective right of veto. A leading example is the EU which, in 2005, saw its proposed Constitution founder on the refusal of two of its member states to ratify the amendment containing it. Amendment of the UN Charter will require the approval of the five permanent members of the Security Council, a requirement which makes Security Council reform rather unlikely.

intense use of the implied powers doctrine; under appeal to the possible legal effect of subsequent practice;[64] or through the adoption of internal policy papers or strategic documents.

A classic example of such informal amendment is offered by NATO's make-over after the fall of communism. Where purists may have insisted on formal amendment of its constitution in order to endow NATO with new tasks, NATO effectively underwent dramatic constitutional change via the non-constitutional way of adopting strategy documents, underlining the accuracy of the proposition that if all members agree that a certain cause of action is imperative, the law of international organizations is ill-equipped to prevent this cause of action from happening.[65]

2.5   Privileges and immunities

One of the consequences of functionalist theory is the idea that if organizations are to exercise their functions effectively, they should be allowed to work without any interference. Over time, the insight grew that this could best be realized by carving out a special position for the organization on the territory of its host state (and the territories of other member states), and the legal technique to do so takes the form of providing for "privileges and immunities". These privileges and immunities are best seen as practical exceptions to the host state's jurisdiction. The host state's laws continue to also apply to the organization, but the organization is protected by a legal shield: the host state's laws cannot be enforced against the organization. Thus, an international organization based in Germany remains in principle subject to German law (including tax law, administrative law, private law, and criminal law) but German law cannot be enforced without

---

64 This was confirmed by the ICJ in *Legal Consequences for States of the Continued Presence of South Africa in Namibia (South West Africa) notwithstanding Security Council Resolution 276 (1970)*, advisory opinion, [1971] ICJ Reports 16. The ICJ confirmed that the practice which had arisen within the Security Council to treat abstentions by permanent members (whose "concurrent vote" is required for most decision-making, under article 27(3) UN Charter) as not blocking the decision-making process, had come to be accepted as legally valid.

65 Useful on NATO's development is Stefan Bölingen, *Die Transformation der NATO im Spiegel der Vertragsentwicklung: Zwischen sicherheitspolitischen Herausforderungen und völkerrechtlicher Legitimität* (2007). The classic monograph on amendment is by Zacklin, who already predicted almost half a century ago that informal amendment (of the sort engaged in by NATO) might be of great practical relevance. See Ralph Zacklin, *The Amendment of the Constitutive Instruments of the United Nations and Specialized Agencies* (1968).

the organization's permission. The underlying rationale holds that if the German police could simply enter the premises and arrest the Director-General, or impose a hefty tax on the organization's income, the organization would be hampered in the exercise of its functions.[66]

The first international organizations, being financed and staffed by the host state, did not know any privileges and immunities, and quite possibly would not have known what to do with them at any rate. The League of Nations Covenant, however, already provided for protection of some individuals as if they were diplomats, and held that the premises of the League were inviolable. This then continued after the Second World War, when privileges and immunities for international organizations came to be generally accepted.[67]

There are no general rules of international law on privileges and immunities: every organization (or cluster of organizations) will have to negotiate its own set of rules with its member states and, in particular, its host state. Typically, such treaties on privileges and immunities will address four distinct groups of subjects. First, such a treaty will protect the *organization* itself, for instance by proclaiming that its premises and archives are inviolable, that it shall be exempt from regular taxation, and that it cannot be sued.[68] Second, the *staff of the organization* will be protected, again in the form of immunities from suit and taxation but also through such things as exemption from visa requirements and military service in the host state. Third, treaties on privileges and immunities need to carve out a special regime for *representatives of member states*, in particular those who travel to and from meetings of the organization. It would be awkward if, on his way to a summit meeting of NATO, the US Defense Secretary could be arrested by Belgian police or, more likely perhaps, if North Korea's representative to the UN could be arrested in the US while travelling to the annual meeting of the General Assembly. While some individuals may be protected by general international law by virtue of their office (heads of state in particular), many others need additional

---

66 The most sophisticated functionalist discussion is P.H.F. Bekker, *The Legal Position of Intergovernmental Organizations: A Functional Necessity Analysis of their Legal Status and Immunities* (1994).

67 See generally Joseph Kunz, "Privileges and Immunities of International Organizations", (1947) 41 *American Journal of International Law* 828–62. The leading monograph on judicial attitudes towards international organizations is August Reinisch, *International Organizations before National Courts* (2000).

68 The EU is exceptional, in that it allows itself to be sued.

protection through conventions on privileges and immunities of international organizations. Fourth, some conventions recognize that there is a category of people that are neither regular staff of the organization nor member state representatives. The 1946 Convention on Privileges and Immunities of the UN refers to this category of people as *experts on mission*, and the ICJ has held that the group comprises a wide variety of individuals, ranging from peacekeeping soldiers to rapporteurs of UN bodies and organs.[69]

It is arguable that under international law all organizations can claim a right to enjoy at least some degree of privileges and immunities, but the precise scope of privileges and immunities is always subject to negotiations. Such negotiations involve at least the organization and its host state (well-nigh all organizations have a headquarters agreement with the state in which they have their headquarters) and, within the host state, typically a broad group of authorities. Thus, the negotiating partner will comprise, at least, the state's foreign ministry, but also its tax authorities (because of taxation exemptions); its labour authorities (because of work permit issues, including possibly those of spouses of staff members); and its immigration authorities (related to visa requirements and residence permits).

Headquarters agreements with the host state tend to be very detailed, fleshing out the more general provisions laid down either in a general convention (such as the 1946 Convention on the Privileges and Immunities of the UN) or even in a single provision in the constituent document (such as article 104 of the UN Charter) – or both.[70] In addition to these instruments (constitution, general convention, headquarters agreement), many states enact their own legislation to give effect to these international instruments. In the UK and the US, for instance, local legislation specifies in varying ways that privileges and immunities come to be applicable to an organization once the government has indicated that they shall become so applicable. This serves, so to speak, as governmental recognition of the organization in question. In some cases, domestic law may also be the main source of privileges and immunities. This applies, for example, in Finland to meetings of specific organizations taking place in Finland: a general law, listing a number of organizations by name, specifies that individuals attending

---

69 See *Applicability of Article VI, Section 22, of the Convention on the Privileges and Immunities of the United Nations*, advisory opinion, [1989] ICJ Reports 177.

70 The leading study is A.S. Muller, *International Organizations and their Host States* (1995).

the meeting shall enjoy privileges and immunities for the duration of the meeting and while travelling to and from the meeting.

Most instruments on the privileges and immunities of international organizations build in the caveat that the privileges and immunities only apply to official acts of the organization, so practically the most relevant question is often the question: who decides? In the limited circumstances of a UN special rapporteur being imprisoned for words spoken in an interview, the ICJ made clear that, in the context of the UN, great weight shall be given to the opinion of the UN Secretary-General: if the Secretary-General feels that someone acted in an official capacity, than this creates a presumption that can only be set aside "for the most compelling reasons".[71] The other side of the coin, of course, is that officials and organizations must act responsibly: the Court ended its discussion in this case by stipulating that "all agents of the United Nations, in whatever official capacity they act, must take care not to exceed the scope of their functions".[72]

Since the opinion of the organization itself weighs so heavily when it comes to assessing the scope of the notion of official act, many have observed that the law on privileges and immunities is tilted in favour of the organization. This causes particular problems when the organization is implicated in human suffering. A recent, prominent example is the outbreak of cholera in Haiti, almost certainly caused by UN peacekeepers from Nepal, deployed in Haiti in the aftermath of the 2010 earthquake. Since then, some 8,000 people have died, and over 100,000 have fallen ill. The issue then obviously arises whether the UN can be sued in order to compensate, and this creates complicated legal questions. One question is whether the UN actually violated any international legal rules – this is uncertain. First, the UN did not order cholera to break out. Second, the UN could be accused of negligence if the peacekeepers were never tested or if sanitation was less than it should have been, but this is unclear as a matter of fact.[73]

But regardless of whether the UN's acts and omissions would have violated international law, it is clear that the UN can claim immunity

---

71 See *Difference Relating to Immunity from Legal Process of a Special Rapporteur of the Commission of Human Rights*, advisory opinion, [1999] ICJ Reports 62, para. 61.

72 See *Difference Relating to Immunity*, para. 66.

73 The otherwise excellent book by Katz becomes a bit opaque on this point, suggesting rather than demonstrating that no testing of peacekeepers had taken place. See Jonathan M. Katz, *The Big Truck That Went By: How the World Came to Save Haiti and Left Behind a Disaster* (2013).

for official acts.[74] How then to classify the unintentional outbreak of cholera? Surely, the UN is not in the business of spreading disease, so the act itself cannot be seen as "official". Equally clearly though, the UN was also not acting in a private or non-official capacity when cholera broke out; hence, the very dichotomy between official and unofficial acts is less than useful here. The 1946 Convention on Privileges and Immunities provides that the UN shall make an effort to settle private claims, the background of this provision probably being that otherwise, no service providers would want to engage with the UN. Providers of a commercial service do not want to run the risk of not getting paid and not even being allowed to sue when they are not getting paid. But opinions are divided whether compensation claims by relatives of victims can be considered as private claims.[75]

Amidst all the uncertainty, what is abundantly clear is that the UN is not doing itself any favours by refusing to apologize. It has steadfastly maintained a deafening silence, insisting that any claim relating to the cholera in Haiti involves a policy evaluation, and has refused to accept any kind of responsibility for the outbreak. Perhaps it has felt compelled to do so for legal reasons, on the theory that any admission of responsibility might be used against it in court. Be that as it may, it is clear that something tragic happened on the UN's watch and with UN involvement, and many agree that its refusal even to apologize constitutes a moral failure.

The episode once more suggests that, in particular when human rights (broadly conceived) are at issue, the immunity of international organizations can be seen as problematic.[76] Surely, violating human rights cannot be part of the official acts of the organization, but neither can the violation of human rights be considered a private or non-official act. In the context of labour disputes (where the rights of staff members of international organizations are at issue) this has prompted the

---

74 The UN's immunity (and that of its Secretary-General) was upheld in a suit related to the cholera outbreak in Haiti by the US District Court for the Southern District of New York in *Delama Georges and others* v. *United Nations and others*, decision of 9 January 2015, available at www.ijdh. org/wp-content/uploads/2011/11/Dkt62_Opinion_and_Order_01_09_15.pdf (visited 23 January 2015).

75 For a rich and balanced discussion, see Frédéric Mégrét, "La responsabilité des Nations Unies aux temps du choléra", (2013) *Revue Belge du Droit International* 161–89.

76 The seminal article is Michael Singer, "Jurisdictional Immunity of International Organizations: Human Rights and Functional Necessity Concerns", (1995) 36 *Virginia Journal of International Law* 53–165.

European Court of Human Rights (ECtHR) to intervene in a set of cases, spearheaded by its decision in *Waite and Kennedy*.[77] At issue was the question of access to justice. In the absence of a staff tribunal and given the general immunity of organizations from suit, disgruntled employees of international organizations have nowhere to turn to, and are thus denied their human right to have access to justice. While the Strasbourg Court was willing to accept that international organizations are a force for good and thus the immunity of organizations is in principle justifiable, immunity should not result in a denial of access to justice to their employees. Hence, organizations are under a general duty to provide some kind of access to justice to staff members, and typically do so either by setting up an administrative tribunal or appeals board of their own, or by accepting the jurisdiction of an existing administrative tribunal. The most generally accepted tribunal is the one originally set up by the League of Nations and now commonly known as the ILO Administrative Tribunal (ILOAT): some 60 organizations have accepted the jurisdiction of ILOAT over disputes with their staff members.

2.6   Dissolution, succession, adaptation

It does not happen too often, but sometimes organizations disappear, usually because the circumstances behind their creation no longer exist. Most famously, the League of Nations was formally dissolved in 1946, having been more or less replaced by the UN. Several organizations in Eastern Europe ceased to exist after the end of communism. Both the Warsaw Pact (the East's answer to NATO) and the Council for Mutual Economic Assistance (COMECON, the East's answer to the EU) were dissolved in the early 1990s: their usefulness as vehicles for communist cooperation had come to an end. The dissolution of organizations provokes several legal questions, concerning both procedure and substance. The procedural question is this: who gets to decide on dissolution? Is that the organization itself and, if so, which of its organs? Or is that decision reserved for the member states acting together but by-passing the organization? The advantage of leaving it to the plenary organ of the organization itself is that this usually makes it easier: the plenary can typically decide by some kind of majority vote, with the result that no single state can veto the dissolution. By contrast,

---

77 See Application No. 26083/94, *Waite and Kennedy* v. *Germany*, ECtHR, judgment of 18 February 1999.

if left to all members together, each and every one of them has a veto, and can thus obstruct the dissolution deemed so desirable by everyone else.[78]

Substantive questions relate to the fate of staff, assets and debts of the organization. Here much will depend on whether there will be a new organization replacing the earlier one. If so (think of the relationship between the League of Nations and the UN), the new entity can take over staff members, assets, debts and tasks of the disappearing one. Strict succession is probably non-existent: even the League and the UN co-existed for some time, which implies that the UN cannot be seen as the successor to the legal rights and obligations of the League. As a result, much is regulated on the basis of agreement between the vanishing organization and the newly created institution: often such agreement will specify what happens to staff, assets and debts, while the tasks of the newcomer will be spelled out in its constituent document.[79]

Sometimes a different technique is chosen: instead of discarding an existing organization and creating a new one from scratch, a new entity is grafted onto the framework of an existing one. This has the benefit that acquired rights can remain in place, although the drawback may well be that the non-functioning elements of the *ancien régime* cannot be shaken off and will be imported into the new organization. In this fashion, the WTO was built on the skeleton of the GATT, and the EU on top of the existing European Community.

Most organizations are created for an indefinite period of time, but there are exceptions. Most well-known perhaps was the case of the European Community for Coal and Steel, initially envisaged to exist for a period of 50 years and indeed largely dismantled when those 50 years had passed, except for some small parts that were transferred to the EU. Less well-known is the exceptional case of the Financial Action Task Force, an organization (housed within the OECD) dealing with such issues as money laundering and based on specific mandates that are formulated for a specific and limited period of time.

---

78 This is putting the matter a bit too strongly perhaps for practical purposes. If a single member state obstructs the dissolution of an organization then the organization continues to exist on paper, but will not have much of a life in practice.

79 The leading monograph is Patrick R. Myers, *Succession between International Organizations* (1993).

Organizations may disappear once their tasks are no longer considered relevant, but obviously this need not be the case: sometimes the organization can re-invent itself, and the most relevant case in point is NATO. With the end of communism and the fall of the Berlin wall, NATO in an important sense lost its *raison d'être*. It had been set up as a defensive alliance against the communist danger, and now the communist danger had disappeared. But, as mentioned, instead of NATO therewith being dismantled, it adopted a number of strategy documents positioning itself as something of a global police force, useful in peace enforcement operations and, as it turned out, the war on terror which erupted after 2001. NATO has been active in the former Yugoslavia, in Afghanistan, and in fighting piracy off the coast of Somalia, to name some examples.

2.7   The nature of international organizations

International organizations typically are set up to perform a function, and to this end, again typically, have been given certain powers, but there is a great variety in the amount and reach of powers granted. On one end, the EU has been granted powers that can directly intervene in the legal order of the member states: the EU can make legislation on, say, the use of chemicals in the workplace, or the ways European firms should behave. By contrast, other organizations have fairly limited powers: the European Forestry Institute, a small research-based entity headquartered in Joensuu, in the east of Finland, can take decisions related to forestry research, but not much more. More surprisingly perhaps, given its global prominence, the WTO has very few powers: it can grant member states permission to depart from free trade rules if they have a good reason (in other words, the WTO can waive member obligations[80]) and has a well-developed system to help solve trade disputes, but it lacks specific policy-making and legislative powers.

To the extent that organizations have such policy-related powers, they are often depicted as places of action. Yet, organizations are also often depicted as glorified debating clubs. It is no coincidence that the WTO's predecessor, the GATT, is sometimes, half-jokingly, referred to as the General Agreement to Talk and Talk, or that people quip that the United Nations Conference on Trade and Development

---

80 The seminal study is Isabel Feichtner, *The Law and Politics of WTO Waivers: Stability and Flexibility in Public International Law* (2012).

(UNCTAD) stands for Under No Circumstance Take Any Decision.[81] While it may be tempting to dismiss this role as inconsequential, by serving as fora for debate and discussion organizations help construct the social world.[82]

In fact, most organizations find themselves on a continuum between the two poles of action and deliberation or, as it has been called, between a managerial concept and an *agora* concept of international organization.[83] Every single organization will display elements of both, which helps explain why we can sometimes both chide the UN for doing too much and for doing too little. If the UN is blamed for not intervening during the Rwandan genocide, it is usually from a managerial perspective: from such a perspective, after all, the UN should solve problems. If, on the other hand, the UN is blamed for imposing sanctions on individuals without due concern for their human rights,[84] then the critics are inspired rather by an *agora* concept: the idea that the UN is a place where people can meet, exchange information and ideas, and hope to solve their problems through discussion, debate and deliberation. From such a perspective, the UN should take action only upon serious reflection and deliberation – and not just for the sake of taking action.

---

81 A little less cleverly perhaps, OECD is sometimes said to stand for Office for Excellent Cocktails and Dinners.

82 See generally Ian Johnstone, *The Power of Deliberation: International Law, Politics and Organizations* (2011).

83 See Jan Klabbers, "Two Concepts of International Organization", (2005) 2 *International Organizations Law Review* 277–93. The idea is gratefully borrowed from the work of political philosopher Michael Oakeshott, who pioneered a similar distinction in connection with state formation. See Michael Oakeshott, *On Human Conduct* (1975).

84 The leading study on the work of UN sanctions committees is Jeremy Matam Farrall, *United Nations Sanctions and the Rule of Law* (2007). A sophisticated argument holding that some actions by the Security Council may even lawfully result in states taking countermeasures is Antonios Tzanakopoulos, *Disobeying the Security Council: Counter-measures against Wrongful Sanctions* (2011).

3 International organizations and their members

3.1 Introduction

All organizations will have some rules concerning who is allowed to join them. This only makes sense: they are not like commercial clubs striving for as large a membership as possible, but are, at least in theory, devoted to a particular function or set of functions. It follows that many organizations will accept as member states those states that can contribute (or can be expected to contribute) to the performance of these functions, and might resist applications from those that do not.

For states, joining organizations might be of interest for various reasons. With some organizations, the attraction resides precisely in the functions exercised by the organization. Thus, states join WIPO if they are interested in taking advantage of the global intellectual property regime, and they join the WTO if they feel that being part of the global trade regime will be useful to them. Likewise, it would be difficult to run a modern airline sector and have modern airports without joining ICAO. It is also on this functionalist basis that applicants can be refused. One example is that Liechtenstein was barred from joining the League of Nations in 1920 precisely because, not having its own army, it was considered incapable of contributing to the League's functioning which, after all, involved a system of collective security. In regional organizations, the functioning is inextricably linked to the location: Israel and Morocco are considered unable to contribute to the EU's goals precisely because they are not located in Europe.

In many cases, however, the benefits are mostly intangible. Thus, states want to join the UN not so much because they get something substantive out of it, but because UN membership bestows a form of collective recognition on the state. This helps explain the discussions over Palestine's application constantly being blocked: many are sympathetic to the idea of Palestinian statehood, but unless and until Palestine joins the UN, doubts about its statehood will remain, even if it is accepted as a member state of other organizations. Membership of the UN has come to be regarded as synonymous to membership of the international community, and is as good an indicator of statehood as any.[85]

Something similar applies, if less strongly, to EU membership in Europe: while there may be concrete benefits to EU membership (agricultural subsidies, for example), there may also be heavy financial burdens involved (think of bailing out other members in trouble). The attraction then resides less in economic benefits than in intangibles: the sense of being admitted to a community of fate. For many of the eastern European states who joined the EU in 2004 and beyond, much of the attraction must have been that membership closed the door on a troubled past: joining the EU means saying a final goodbye to Russia, and a state such as Finland (which joined in 1995 and shares a long border with Russia) was no doubt in part inspired by the idea that a Russian invasion of an EU member state would demand a collective EU response. Hence, the EU treaty was seen to contain an implied promise of collective security.[86]

Most organizations have some rules on how new members can join; some organizations also have rules on suspension or expulsion of member states. Thus, the UN can, according to article 6 of the UN Charter, expel a state which has "persistently violated" the principles laid down in the UN Charter. To date, however, this has never happened, and the reason will be obvious: expelling a state also means that the organization will forfeit any leverage it has over that state. Put differently, expelling state X from membership most likely also implies that the organization cannot impose any sanctions on state X, and will be less well-placed to try and persuade state X to behave more appropriately. That is not to say expulsions do not take place: a celebrated example is the expulsion of the Soviet Union from the League of Nations in 1939, after it had invaded Finland.

In addition to expulsion, the UN Charter also provides that member state rights may be suspended. Under article 19, this applies in par-

---

85 See John Dugard, *Recognition and the United Nations* (1987).
86 Nowadays, since Lisbon, the promise is more or less explicit. Under the "solidarity clause" of article 222 TFEU, the EU and its members shall jointly respond to terrorist threats and natural and man-made disasters. Despite not being very outspoken, the language is broad enough to also cover foreign invasions and attacks.

ticular to voting rights in the General Assembly of the UN: a state's voting rights may be suspended if the state is in arrears in the payment of its membership contribution for more than two full years. However, even this is seen as a strong medicine, possibly too strong to be applied consistently: especially when powerful member states are in arrears, the compromise solution often reached is to stop voting altogether and instead engage in decision-making by consensus: since consensus as a decision-making technique does not require voting,[87] there is no need to insist on suspension of voting rights.

The League of Nations contained, in its very opening article, a clause on withdrawal by member states. Given the experiences of the League, when Germany and Japan both withdrew in the 1930s following accusations of aggressive policies, the drafters of the UN Charter decided against inclusion of a withdrawal clause, and to date no state has withdrawn from the UN. There is one example of a possible withdrawal: in the mid-1960s, Indonesia announced its withdrawal after its neighbour state, Malaysia, had been elected to serve on the Security Council. Indonesia felt this was an affront – it had territorial disputes with Malaysia, and felt that Malaysia's election meant the UN had taken sides. Still, Indonesia never formally withdrew, and returned to the UN after a number of months; the episode is often taken as an example of Indonesia's non-participation rather than withdrawal.

3.2 Admission

There are no general rules of international law on admission, neither on the substantive requirements nor on the procedure to be followed. As a result, every constitution will provide its own sets of rules, and much will depend on such things as whether the organization is open to universal membership or closed, and on the ambitions of the organization's policies.

The UN has become a by-word for an open organization, and since the mid-1950s has adopted a policy of admitting all states that want to

---

87 Consensus signifies that a conclusion is reached that raises no strong objections from anyone. It is technically to be distinguished from decision-making by unanimity, although in practice the two are often indistinguishable: employing consensus, all member states effectively hold a veto, which they might be inclined to give up in favour of concessions on some topic or another. There is, therewith, a strong linkage between consensus and package deals.

join, provided only that they are, indeed, states.[88] Article 4 of the UN Charter posits a number of substantive requirements: the UN is open to states; those states must be peace-loving, and must be able and willing to carry out the obligations that come with membership.

When in the late 1940s the Cold War broke out, this was reflected in the admission practices of the UN: Western states were reluctant to accept communist states as new members; the UN's communist member states in turn were reluctant to admit Western states into membership, and a well-known stalemate ensued. This raised the question whether blocking applications could be done for political reasons, or whether the criteria mentioned in article 4 are exhaustive. The question reached the ICJ, which, in a somewhat Delphic opinion, held that the criteria of article 4 are exhaustive, but obviously demand interpretation. It could not prohibit states from taking political factors into account, all it could (and did) say was that member states must interpret the criteria of article 4 in good faith.[89]

This did little to solve the crisis, and two years later a new question was brought to the Court, this time focusing on procedure. Part of the problem with all those frozen applications was that the five permanent members of the Security Council[90] have a right to veto applications. Under article 4, decisions on admission shall be made by the General Assembly, upon recommendation by the Security Council. Hence, some in the General Assembly felt that despite a negative vote by the Security Council, the Assembly could nonetheless admit an aspiring new member, as the hallmark of a recommendation is that it is not binding. The Court was asked whether the Assembly could admit new member states despite the absence of a Council recommendation, but the Court answered in the negative. It held that the procedure envisaged created a balance between the two organs, and that this balance had to be respected.[91] If the Council recommends a state, the

---

88 For a critique, arguing that the UN has become too relaxed in admitting new member states, see Thomas D. Grant, *Admission to the United Nations: Charter Article 4 and the Rise of Universal Organization* (2009).

89 See *Conditions of Admission of a State to Membership in the United Nations (Article 4 of the Charter)*, advisory opinion, [1948] ICJ Reports 57.

90 These are the US, the UK, France, China and, as the Charter still holds, the USSR.

91 See *Competence of the General Assembly for the Admission of a State to the United Nations*, advisory opinion, [1950] ICJ Reports 4. See generally also Jan Klabbers, "Checks and Balances in the Law of International Organizations", in Mortimer Sellers (ed.), *Autonomy in the Law* (2007), 141–63.

Assembly can still decide against that state; but it cannot act without recommendation. It follows that all applicant member states need to pass the first hurdle of the Security Council, and thus need to meet with the approval (or at least not active resistance) of the five permanent members. In practice, this entails that an entity such as Palestine shall not be admitted unless and until the US gives up its resistance, and given the close ties between the US and Israel this is unlikely to happen any time soon. Likewise, any application by Taiwan will have to overcome Chinese opposition, while an application by Kosovo is likely to be blocked by Serbia's staunchest ally, Russia.

Since the Court was unable to solve the political crisis, a political compromise had to be found, and was eventually reached in 1955, when East and West agreed to accept states regardless of which ideological camp they belonged to,[92] and in the intervening years the UN has almost quadrupled from its original 50 member states to its current tally of 193 member states – the latest to join was newly independent South Sudan in 2011.

In some organizations, membership is tied to membership of another organization. Thus, the ILO has an easier admission procedure for states that have been admitted to the UN than for others, and membership of the IMF is even a pre-condition for joining the World Bank. Most organizations are still only open to states – after all, it is a defining element of international organizations that they are created by states. Still, there are exceptions. The WTO has accepted entities that have their own customs authorities: Hong Kong, Taiwan and Macao are all members of the WTO, even if they are not generally considered states in their own right. A historical aberration was that during the days of the USSR, two of its constituent republics were independently also members of the UN: Ukraine and Belarus. This is usually ascribed to Stalin's plan to stack the UN with members on whose support he could rely, and only met a limit when the US threatened to do the same: the 50 states of the US would easily outnumber the 15 of the USSR.

A special case is the EU, which has been accepted as a member by some organizations despite not being considered a state. The EU's member states have granted certain competences to the EU in fields such as international trade and fisheries, so much so that these competences

---

92 A good discussion of these issues is Bengt Broms, *The Doctrine of Equality of States as Applied in International Organizations* (1959).

are exercised in an exclusive manner: the member states of the EU have no authority left in these matters. It follows that the EU has an interest in joining organizations such as the WTO or the North Atlantic Fisheries Organization: if the EU is exclusively competent in these matters, then it feels it should also be allowed to participate in relevant organizations – it is reluctant to leave matters (re-delegate, so to speak) to its member states. Some organizations have agreed to this: the WTO has accepted the EU as one of its founding members, and the FAO has changed its constitution to accommodate EU membership. Others have not: the EU holds some (small) exclusive powers relating to safety in the workplace, but is unable to join the ILO: as mentioned, one needs to be a UN member before one can join the ILO, and the UN only accepts states. And whatever the EU is at present, it is not a state. In such a case, then, the EU court has reminded member states that they have a duty of cooperation within the ILO, and are expected to represent the EU interest above and beyond their individual interests when acting within the ILO.[93]

EU membership itself is very demanding: the effects of EU law in the domestic legal orders of the member states are so strong that member states are expected prior to joining to prepare their legal orders for the influence of EU law. The EU has strict rules on competition law, for example, as well as on state aids and government procurement. Citizens of EU member states can travel throughout the EU looking for work, or retire to another member state and bring their pensions with them. In short, on many issues of everyday life the EU exerts a strong influence. Hence, aspiring member states are usually expected to spend a number of years in the waiting room (the antechamber) on the basis of an association agreement: this way, they can adapt to the exigencies of EU law prior to their actual joining. Much of the details will eventually be regulated in so-called accession agreements, which need to be accepted unanimously by the EU's existing membership, including the relevant domestic authorities of all existing member states. It takes many years and considerable detail to negotiate these agreements – joining the EU is not done on a whim.

That said, not all associations result in membership eventually. Sometimes the association agreement is used as a substitute for membership, for instance when the state in question is located outside Europe but still considered to be a useful partner (Israel, Morocco), or

---

93 See *Opinion 2/91 (ILO)* [1993] ECR I-1061.

when not everyone is equally enthusiastic about the state in question. This helps explain why Turkey has had associate status with the EU for already half a century but is no closer to full membership. Some argue that Turkey is not "really" European; others fear a mass influx of poor migrants, and yet others worry about the impact a secular state largely composed of Muslims would have on Europe's proclaimed Christian values and character. Some also point out that Turkey's human rights record is not on the level one might hope for in a member state of the EU.

The EU is not the only organization with a lengthy and complicated admission procedure. While the effect of the WTO on domestic law is far less pronounced than that of the EU, nonetheless the WTO has a clear ideology – that of the free market. In particular, states whose markets have been strongly regulated therefore need to engage in serious negotiations with the WTO before being admitted, precisely in order to adapt to the free market – both China and Russia went through lengthy accession negotiations before they joined the WTO.

3.3   Financing

Member states owe their organizations a general good faith duty of obedience, but typically this does not come with a great deal of specific legal obligations. There is an expectation that a member state will participate in meetings of organs and subsidiary organs, but not normally speaking a strict legal obligation. There is an expectation that recommendations issued by the organization will be considered in good faith by the competent domestic authorities, but not much more than this unless the organization has explicit law-making powers. However, the one obligation that often comes with membership is to contribute to the finances of the organization: most organizations (though not all) insist that their member states pay a regular membership fee. If this is one of the few obligations on members accompanying membership, it also grants member states an instrument of power: withholding the contribution can cause the organization considerable harm.[94]

The financial provisions can be rather innocuous in formulation. Article 17(2) of the UN Charter, for example, merely provides that

---

94 The classic study is José E. Alvarez, "Legal Remedies and the United Nations' à la Carte Problem", (1991) 12 *Michigan Journal of International Law* 229–311.

the UN's expenses "shall be borne by the Members as apportioned by the General Assembly". Nonetheless, its innocuous formulation notwithstanding, there are two important ramifications. First, there is a legal obligation to contribute. Second, the budgetary power rests with the General Assembly. In case a member state defaults, sanctions are envisaged: under article 19, a member state that is in arrears for more than two years "shall have no vote in the General Assembly". In reality, though, the sanction does not set in automatically: the Assembly may grant the defaulting member state the right to vote after all, and the Assembly may decide not to resort to voting at all but instead to decide by consensus.

The UN is often in a situation of financial crisis. The membership fees, as apportioned by the General Assembly, are roughly based on gross national income, the basic idea being that the richest member states shall contribute the most. This, however, would imply that the UN would be hugely dependent on the US, and as this is deemed undesirable (it would give the US the power to bring the UN to a standstill), a ceiling has been established with respect to the US contribution, and has been regularly adjusted: the US shall contribute no more than some 22 per cent of the UN's regular budget. Even this is far, far more than the next biggest contributors: Japan, the second-biggest contributor, contributes a little under 11 per cent, whereas Germany, in third, contributes a little over 7 per cent to the regular budget. Remarkably, with the exception of the US, the permanent members of the Security Council are not amongst the really big contributors: France, the UK and China each take care of a little over 5 per cent, and Russia a paltry 2.5 per cent, of the regular budget.

In a landmark decision, the ICJ held in 1962 that peacekeeping, even if not envisaged anywhere in the Charter, nonetheless is a legitimate task of the UN, and accordingly found that peacekeeping expenses can be part of the regular budget.[95] This overcame Russian and French objections – these member states, both permanent members of the Security Council, had been of the opinion that peacekeeping as authorized by the General Assembly would undermine the position of the Security Council. Still, despite the *Certain Expenses* opinion, peacekeeping operations usually have their own budgets, and it is usually the case that the richer member states pay while operations are carried out by poorer member states. Again, the US pays for the lion's share of

---

95 See *Certain Expenses*.

peacekeeping operations, followed at a respectable distance by Japan, France and Germany.

In addition to member state income, many organizations also rely on voluntary contributions, either by private benefactors or by member states. The latter option is attractive for member states since it implies that they can also dictate what their money will be spent on. This way they can sponsor pet projects and do not have to stand by idly while the organization is spending income on activities the member state concerned does not agree with.

Organizations can also generate income from their activities. UNICEF, as is well known, sells Christmas cards and receives donations from football club Barcelona CF; WIPO provides advice on intellectual property matters for a fee; while ICAO does much the same when it comes to airport security.

The EU has a peculiar system, referred to, somewhat misleadingly perhaps, as a system of "own resources". The Treaty on the Functioning of the European Union (TFEU) provides that the EU shall have its own resources, and that the Council shall elaborate this in a further instrument.[96] The decision currently in force goes back to 2007,[97] and specifies that the EU's own resources shall consist of import duties, a percentage of domestic value-added tax income of the member states, and a percentage of the gross national income of the member states. Notwithstanding the grievances of populist politicians, while the absolute sums involved may be large, the percentages are modest, and the total amount of gross national income that states should contribute (this comprises their contribution from all three types of resources) is set at a little over 1 per cent of gross national income.

Typically, organizational expenses fall into two categories: administrative and operational, and it depends on the sort of organization which is the bigger category. Peacekeeping operations or the running of refugee camps cost a lot of money, so with organizations such as the UN or the UNHCR a substantial amount is spent on operational costs. Organizations that do not engage in such activities "on the ground", however, will have less operational costs; the percentage of administrative costs will be higher.

---

96 See article 311 TFEU.
97 Council Decision 2007/436 EC, Euratom.

3.4   Withdrawal

In the functionalist theory of the law of international organizations, withdrawal is often seen as an option to be exercised when the organization is not, or not adequately, or no longer, performing its functions. Consequently, some constitutional documents contain a withdrawal clause, allowing states to withdraw upon following a prescribed procedure. Other organizational constitutions, however, lack such a clause, and in that case it is considered an open question whether the member is allowed to withdraw.

Typically, organizations are created on a permanent basis, and the starting assumption is that membership will also remain permanent. Given the number of organizations in existence and the number of states, withdrawals from membership are indeed rare occurrences. Partly this is explained by the classic notion that if you drop out of the game, you also lose the capacity to influence: if you are not playing, you cannot score. Hence, withdrawal is very much an option of last resort, although some politicians revel in threatening to withdraw if and when they do not get their way.

For the same reason, withdrawal is also something that is better suited for powerful states that are not dependent on the tangible or intangible benefits of membership. There are, admittedly, cases of states that have withdrawn for reasons unrelated to direct benefits: Greece, for instance, withdrew from the Council of Europe in the late 1960s just before a complaint against it would be filed under the ECHR; it decided, all things considered, that it was better off outside the Council than being held responsible for human rights violations.

But the more typical examples involve powerful states using the right to withdraw as a way of influencing the organization, in the expectation that the organization has more to lose than the state concerned. A classic example is the US withdrawal from the ILO in 1977, with the US suggesting that the ILO had turned leftist and was pandering to eastern European influence.[98] Another is how the US and the UK both left UNESCO in the mid-1980s amidst accusations of nepotism, corruption and mission creep within the organization. Both have

---

98 See William P. Alford, "The Prospective Withdrawal of the United States from the International Labor Organization: Rationales and Implications", (1976) 17 *Harvard International Law Journal* 623–38. The US returned to the ILO in 1980.

since returned, but not until after the organization went through serious changes.[99] And France creatively left the military structure of NATO in the mid-1960s while remaining part of NATO's political structure, therewith effectively withdrawing French troops from US leadership. This was an unprecedented move on France's part, but met with acquiescence on the part of the rest of NATO's membership.

What these cases have in common is that the state concerned uses its power to express dissatisfaction with the political course of the organization; what they also have in common is that, often, this is not based on strictly legal considerations, but serves as a blunt political instrument. The US and the UK may well have been concerned with mission creep in UNESCO but, as then Director-General M'Bow reminded them, to say that UNESCO's involvement with peace and security meant the organization had run wild, was simply implausible. After all, the UNESCO constitution firmly embeds UNESCO's functioning within the broader framework of peace and security: whatever UNESCO does is meant to further the cause of peace and security, so it becomes disingenuous to accuse the UNESCO of overstepping its mandate. Such withdrawals on the part of member states herewith display two things. First, they testify that the functions of organizations are often drawn up in ambitious and grandiose terms: it is difficult to chide UNESCO for claiming to work for peace and security, even if arguably it ought to focus more on education and culture. Second, they will often display a self-serving element: the US and the UK had some (justifiable) concern over whether UNESCO lived up to its own constituent document, but were also worried about the political course chartered by UNESCO, and those two factors are not always easy to disentangle.

Where the constituent document provides for withdrawal, things are relatively straightforward, legally speaking. Dilemmas may arise, however, when the organization does not formally allow for withdrawal. A first question to address then is whether withdrawal is nonetheless possible. Some answer in the negative, claiming that if the founders had envisaged withdrawal they should have included a provision to that effect. Withdrawal is thought to weaken the organization, therewith undermining it in the performance of its tasks, and thus is

---

99 See Yves Beigbeder, *Management Problems in United Nations Organizations: Reform or Decline?* (1987).

fundamentally irreconcilable with the functionalist nature of international organizations.[100]

Others, more realistically perhaps, have suggested that even if the constitution does not allow for withdrawal, there is little point in keeping reluctant members on board, for there are various ways in which they might come to endanger the functioning of the organization. The reluctant member state can refuse to implement collective decisions, or it can boycott decision-making sessions and thus make unanimity unachievable;[101] in such circumstances, a divorce might be preferable to the continuation of a bad marriage. Whether that means that divorce ought to be invited through inclusion of a withdrawal provision is another matter: quite a few eyebrows were raised when the EU, in its 2009 Lisbon amendments, decided to include such a provision.[102]

A second question relates to procedure. If a constitution allows for withdrawal, it will most likely also provide the procedure for withdrawal, so again the legal situation will be relatively straightforward. However, problems arise if the constitution does not allow for withdrawal. On the one hand, one might suggest that it is then up to the member concerned to decide whether, when, and on what conditions, to withdraw, but such would potentially do an injustice to the organization (and the remaining member states). On the other hand, letting the organization decide would lack a basis in law, and might lead to injustice to the withdrawing member state.

These things assume relevance because there might be concrete material interests at stake. For instance, the IMF can hardly accept the unilateral withdrawal of a member state without guarantees that it will pay back its outstanding loans; the WHO can hardly accept the unilateral withdrawal of a member state in which a contagious disease has just broken out; and the UNHCR might be reluctant to accept the unilateral withdrawal of a state experiencing a large refugee inflow due to a crisis in a neighbouring state. The examples suggest that organizations are not just vehicles for cooperation between states, but can also serve to discipline member states and their citizens.

---

100 For such a claim, see H.G. Schermers, and Niels M. Blokker, *International Institutional Law: Unity Within Diversity* (5th edn., 2011), 98–9.

101 See generally J.H.H. Weiler, "Alternatives to Withdrawal from an International Organization: The Case of the European Economic Community", (1985) 20 *Israel Law Review* 282–98.

102 See article 50 TEU.

3.5 Expulsion, suspension and related techniques

Precisely because organizations can be used as platforms for disciplining states, expulsions are relatively rare. Probably the best-known example is the expulsion of the USSR from the League of Nations after its invasion of Finland in 1939. Other examples remain hard to find, although not for want of trying. Quite a few organizations have tried, for example, to expel the Spain of General Franco in the 1940s and 1950s or South Africa in the days of apartheid. Likewise, Israel has sometimes had to resist attempts at expulsion from organizations, as has Egypt upon making peace with Israel.[103]

The examples suggest that more often than not, expulsion attempts take place for reasons which have not all that much to do with functionalist concerns. Attempts to expel South Africa from UPU in the 1960s had little to do with South Africa's ability or inability to deliver the mail, but had everything to do with its apartheid policies. These were deemed to constitute serious human rights violations, and the sentiment arose that UPU should not collaborate in any way with such a state – South Africa was deemed unworthy of membership.

Understandable as the reasoning is, it is inherently problematic for two reasons. One is pragmatic: on this line of reasoning, few states can be considered worthy members of any international organization. Few states have an unblemished human rights record, by whatever standard, so to insist on respect for human rights as an implied precondition for continued membership may well be lofty, but is bound to be selective, and not all that practical.

The other is a matter of principle: considerations of worthiness are very much in the eye of the beholder, and a matter of political inclination and preference. Admittedly, apartheid met with universal condemnation, so the point can be made that attempts to expel South Africa had universal backing. But the situation becomes more difficult when the position of a state such as Egypt is considered: surely, one may legitimately wonder whether making peace with a neighbouring state can ever be good reason for being ostracized.

---

103 Useful overviews of practice include Konstantinos D. Magliveras, *Exclusion from Participation in International Organisations: The Law and Practice behind Member States' Expulsion and Suspension of Membership* (1999), and Alison Duxbury, *The Participation of States in International Organisations: The Role of Human Rights and Democracy* (2011).

If expulsion is rare, it is somewhat more common that the rights of member states are suspended for some time, again predominantly with a view to having that member state adapt some of its policies. Again, then, the inspiration is political rather than functional, and such suspensions tend to be more convincing with respect to "general" organizations than with respect to strictly functional entities. In other words, to suspend Zimbabwe from the Commonwealth citing human rights concerns is somehow more plausible than a suspension of the same state and for the same reasons from, say, WIPO.

Again, many of the same legal questions arise, for instance, whether suspension is envisaged in the constituent document, whether suspension needs to be done for particular reasons, whether there are conditions to be attached, and what sort of decision-making is to be used. Those are, needless to say, important questions: their existence helps to safeguard both the position of the organization and that of the member state concerned. And yet, those questions are often circumvented or all but ignored: politics quickly takes precedence.

Some organizations have several distinct procedures relating to suspension. The UN, for example, has two. The first, as mentioned earlier, treats suspension as a response by the organization to a member state not paying its contribution, and is to be found in article 19 of the UN Charter. The second procedure is listed in article 5 of the UN Charter: the General Assembly can suspend a member state from rights and privileges if the member state in question is one against which preventive or enforcement action is taken. No examples have occurred, and its position in the Charter suggests that it was meant as a stepping stone for the stronger sanction of expulsion, which is laid down in the next article (article 6 of the UN Charter).

Two further techniques are used by organizations to give a voice to their dissatisfaction with a state's regime or behaviour. The first of these is the clever practice of refusing to accept the credentials of representatives of that state. Typically, before international meetings, a committee is formed to evaluate the credentials of representatives: is Mr X really Mr X, and does he really represent his state and carry instructions from his home government? Obviously, the idea behind the exercise is to bar Mr X from participating if he is not who he claims to be or represent, but the procedure has also been used to bar entire delegations from participating. With respect to South Africa, for example, in various organizations including the UN the credentials procedure has been used to bar South Africa, for if a state's representatives are barred, participation becomes impossible. The legality of the practice may be doubtful (in that it may constitute an abuse of the credentials procedure), but it may be politically expedient. Perhaps the most proper use is when a state is under foreign occupation. When Hungary was invaded by the USSR in 1956, the credentials of some Hungarian delegates were tested, and while a final decision was never made, one observer suggests that the episode displays a willingness on the part of the General Assembly to "question the legitimacy of the authority issuing" the credentials.[104]

Closely related is the insistence on proper representation of the government by the state, and no case is more illustrative than that of China in the UN. When the UN was set up, in 1945, there was only one Chinese government. Later in the 1940s, a revolutionary movement spearheaded by Mao Zedong took power, and the earlier government was driven away, taking refuge on the island of Formosa (Taiwan). For many years, the UN continued to treat the Taiwanese government as the proper representative of China, even if it had become increasingly clear that the real power was exercised by the government run by the communist party of Mao. It took the UN until 1971 to rectify the situation, and since there is, understandably, no procedure for such events envisaged in the Charter, the matter received the shock treatment: while the pertinent General Assembly resolution welcomed delegates from the People's Republic, the Taiwanese delegates were unceremoniously expelled.

3.6   State succession and membership

One of the more complicated issues in international law generally is the question what happens to rights and obligations if a succession of states occurs. This is a complicated matter for at least two reasons. First, the notion of state succession is analytically not very precise. It comprises mergers of existing states, but also secession. It covers decolonization, with all its special political imperatives, but also dissolution of states. Second, each and every single situation tends to be unique. The unification of the two Germanys in the early 1990s was embedded in a political setting that was different from the short-lived merger of Egypt and Syria in 1958 under the name United Arab Republic. The

---

104 See Magliveras, *Exclusion from Participation*, 208.

dissolutions of the Soviet Union and the Socialist Federal Republic of Yugoslavia, while related, were nonetheless dramatically different. In such a setting, few general rules can arise, and in practice much of the relevant issues will have to be hammered out in agreements between the states most closely involved.

As far as membership of international organizations is concerned, there is one general rule: membership is personal.[105] Hence, if a state is replaced by another one, the new state needs to apply for membership. When Czechoslovakia broke up in the early 1990s, its membership of international organizations also came to an end, and the two new states, the Czech Republic and Slovakia, applied for admission of organizations as new states. Likewise, upon seceding from Sudan, the new state of South Sudan had to apply for membership of international organizations. And, should Scotland have seceded from the UK, it too would have had to apply for membership of organizations, including the EU. The rest of the UK, by contrast, would not: its legal identity would remain the same, albeit with a considerably smaller territory.[106]

Still, the rule does not capture situations of merger necessarily, unless the merger is presented as a total novelty. In the case of Germany, for example, the situation was generally treated as one of the disappearance of one state (the erstwhile German Democratic Republic, GDR), and the growth of another (the former Federal Republic of Germany). In other words, the Federal Republic changed its name and expanded its territory, but retained the same legal identity. This did not solve all practical issues: some arrangements had to be made relating to, for example, the outstanding financial contributions of the GDR.

The rule that membership is personal is also subject to political engineering, and the clearest example is the fate of the USSR. Under the "membership is personal" rule, the dissolution of the USSR would have entailed that all former Soviet republics, including Russia, would have lost their membership of organizations. This was considered undesirable: Russia being out of the UN was generally considered a bad idea,

---

105 The leading study is Konrad Bühler, *State Succession and Membership in International Organizations: Legal Theories versus Political Pragmatism* (2001).

106 Note that some of this depends on how the issue is framed. If the Scottish episode would be seen as England, Wales and Northern Ireland departing, then these should apply for membership of organizations.

and even more so because if Russia went, the Security Council would be in trouble. After all, the Charter specifies that Russia (or rather, the USSR, as it still reads) is one of the permanent members. Russia's non-membership would have implied a complete re-thinking of the Council's membership and potentially resulted in huge political instability. Hence, an agreement was quickly reached to treat Russia as the continuation of the former USSR: it changed its name and territory, but not its identity.

By contrast, when Serbia, after the dissolution of Yugoslavia, applied for similar treatment, its appeal was rejected, and in many organizations Serbia had to apply for membership as a new state. This created some problems before the ICJ, with Serbia being on the receiving end of several claims. One of the technical preconditions before a state can be sued before the ICJ is that it must be a party to the ICJ Statute, and that status comes with being a member of the UN. Consequently, a non-member of the UN cannot bring claims against other states, and cannot be on the receiving end of claims either.[107] The ICJ could use this to dismiss cases brought by Serbia over the bombing of Belgrade by NATO member states, but had to twist itself in difficult ways in order to accept a case brought against Serbia – it found a way out in the argument that the case had been brought before Serbia ceased to be a member of the UN, and that in an earlier phase it had already accepted jurisdiction. This decision was *res judicata*, and not to be influenced by later developments.[108] In fact, it was not even certain that Serbia was not a member of the UN: the various political organs of the UN took different decisions, with some thinking Serbia had lost membership, while others construed the episode rather as one of Serbia ceasing to participate, but without losing membership status.[109]

Special considerations are thought to apply to the financial institutions. Since these involve large-scale financial obligations for member states that have borrowed money, it would be problematic if member states could all too easily lose membership status and thus, possibly,

---

107 Unless, quite possibly, it indicates a willingness to bring claims or be sued, but the latter can safely be ignored in the case at hand.

108 See *Application of the Convention on the Prevention and Punishment of the Crime of Genocide (Bosnia and Herzegovina v. Serbia and Montenegro)*, [2007] ICJ Reports 43.

109 A good discussion is Stephan Wittich, "Permissible Derogation from Mandatory Rules? The Problem of Party Status in the Genocide Case", (2007) 18 *European Journal of International Law* 591–618.

also default on their loans. Hypothetically, a state could change its legal identity precisely in order to escape from its debts, and surely this is not considered desirable, however hypothetical the scenario might be. Consequently, with financial institutions, the chosen method is often one of succession by all new states to the obligations of the old one, so as to protect everyone's assets.[110]

---

110 See Paul R. Williams, "State Succession and the International Financial Institutions: Political Criteria v. Protection of Outstanding Financial Obligations", (1994) 43 *International and Comparative Law Quarterly* 766–808.

4 Standard-setting by international organizations

4.1 Introduction

If one of the main reasons why international organizations are set up is to perform a specific function, it follows that they may be expected to set standards relevant to that function. Put simply, if the task of the WHO is to safeguard global public health,[111] then it may be expected that the WHO can at least help define what "global public health" should mean, and may also express some thoughts on how best to achieve global public health. Here, however, a tension may set in with respect to the member states: these may entertain their own ideas as to what "global public health" stands for and how best to achieve it. And those member state ideas may be influenced by a number of domestic factors, ranging from the natural presence of disease-carrying animals on their territory to electoral support by pharmaceutical companies.

As a result, there are at the end of the day not all that many organizations that can actually enact instruments with the effect of law, in other words, general and abstract, applicable to the public at large, and with binding effect – the EU is perhaps the best-known example.[112] In addition, some organizations (or organs thereof) can take administrative decisions: applying pre-existing law to situations brought to their attention. Here the Security Council of the UN is perhaps the most useful illustration. As will be seen, however, the line between law-making and administration is a fine one. A third category of relevant decisions relates to the functioning of the organization itself: organizations need to decide on their budget, on whether or not to admit new member states or expel current ones, and so on. These decisions are usually regarded as being of a household nature: they have to be legally binding by definition (surely, an organization cannot run if all

---

111 The WHO Constitution repeatedly refers to the "health of all peoples".
112 For an authoritative discussion, see Alvarez, *International Organizations*.

its budgetary decisions are merely recommendations), but do not set general and abstract standards. Again, however, the lines between the various categories of instruments are thin and fuzzy. Where organizations do not make or apply the law themselves, they may nonetheless help in the formation of new law by adopting recommendations, or by sponsoring the conclusion of conventions.[113]

4.2 Law-making strictly (and not so strictly) speaking

The most well-known example of an organization with law-making powers is the EU, which can adopt Regulations and Directives, both of which are usually general and binding on the member states. The difference between them is that the Regulation is directly applicable in member state law, whereas Directives by definition require transformation into national law: they set binding targets, but leave the details to the member state legislator. Directives have thus proven very useful in harmonizing the legal systems of the EU member states, while Regulations are the preferred means of creating uniform legislation. In addition, the EU can take so-called Decisions: these are binding on those to whom they are addressed, and thus best seen as exercises of administrative (as opposed to legislative) power.

In addition to the EU, some law-making takes place in the ICAO. States enjoy sovereign jurisdiction over the airspace above their territories and thus, as an important corollary, can also enact legislation relating to that column. The high seas, however, remain outside any state's jurisdiction; hence, legislation concerning air space over the high seas has been left to ICAO.

The WHO also boasts a legislative power: under article 22 of its constitution, its plenary body (the World Health Assembly) can adopt regulations which assume binding force. There is one important caveat, however: states have a right to opt out, and can do so by notifying the Director-General within a limited period of time after adoption of the regulation. The WHO's legislative power has been put to good use when the WHO enacted the so-called International Health Regulations, adopted in 2005 and in force since 2007.

---

113 See generally Laurence R. Helfer, "Nonconsensual International Lawmaking", (2008) *University of Illinois Law Review* 71–125.

A borderline situation of law-making refers again to ICAO, which has the power to adopt standards and recommended practices. The idea here is to legislate by stealth, without being seen to be legislating. The standards and recommended practices become binding law only by implication: states that cannot comply with them are expected immediately to notify this to ICAO. The implication then is that a state that remains silent shall comply.[114] These standards and recommended practices can cover a variety of aspects of air traffic, ranging from the airworthiness of aircraft to the safety of airports and professional qualifications of the crew and ground staff.

Although one would expect the power to set binding standards to arise from the constituent document (this, after all, is the one containing the original act of delegation by states to their organization), some entities derive much of their legislative powers from other instruments. A well-known example refers to the Codex Alimentarius Commission, a joint entity set up by the FAO and the WHO in order to set food safety standards. These led a somewhat dormant existence until the WTO was established, since some of the WTO-related treaties accept the food safety standards developed by the Codex Alimentarius Commission as legal excuses to ban products that do not meet those standards.[115]

A similar development took place, some 20 years earlier, with respect to the International Atomic Energy Agency (IAEA). The IAEA can adopt so-called safeguards under article XII of its constitution, and in the process, for example, prescribe or rely on general health and safety measures. The Non-Proliferation Treaty enhanced the IAEA's status when it linked non-proliferation to oversight by the IAEA: states without nuclear weapons were expected to enter into agreement with the IAEA concerning safeguards relating to nuclear technology and in accordance with the Statute of the IAEA. In other words, standards set by the IAEA could in this way find multiplication.

By the same token, WIPO developed recommendations relating to the use of domain names for the Internet, in 1999. These domain names

---

114 The classic study, now probably a bit outdated, found that states do not always notify departures from ICAO standards and recommendations, even if they do not comply. See Thomas Buergenthal, *Law-making in the International Civil Aviation Organization* (1969).

115 See in particular the Agreement on Sanitary and Phytosanitary Measures (SPS Agreement). It does the same with respect to standards set by the much older International Office of Epizootics. The seminal study of the Codex Alimentarius Commission is Mariëlle Masson-Mathee, *The Codex Alimentarius Commission and Its Standards* (2007).

are not themselves laid down in a binding WIPO document, but were made available to the Internet Corporation for Assigned Names and Numbers (ICANN), which effectively governs the Internet. Hence, the WIPO recommendations manifest a stronger legal force than might be expected solely on the basis of WIPO's constitution.

And in a similar manner, many IMO standards (relating to safety of navigation or marine pollution, for example) have acquired additional force through reference in the UN Convention on the Law of the Sea (UNCLOS). This convention instructs its parties to formulate rules and standards through competent organizations,[116] and it is clear that in maritime matters the IMO qualifies as such. Hence, despite the absence of a legislative power in the IMO's constituent document, the status of IMO standards is upgraded through incorporation in UNCLOS.[117]

4.3   Administration

As noted, the EU, in particular its Commission, engages in what can best be described as the application of pre-existing law by an administrative body. The EU Commission can, for example, impose fines on companies that it deems are violating the anti-trust rules embodied in EU law. Those companies can then ask the courts of the EU (the General Court, in first instance) to review the decision, and perhaps annul it in whole or in part. In the same spirit, the Commission can also take administrative decisions against individual member states, or even the member states collectively. The point to note is twofold. First, those decisions bind only their addressees. Second, they are not to be confused with legislation: they remain limited to the application of pre-existing rules to a specific factual situation.

The UN Security Council was set up to do something similar under the famous Chapter VII of the UN Charter. If the Security Council observes the existence of a threat to the peace, breach of the peace, or act of aggression, it can order a variety of measures.[118] It can, for

---

116   See for example, article 197 UNCLOS.

117   Outdated but analytically useful is Edward Yemin, *Legislative Powers in the United Nations and Specialized Agencies* (1969).

118   These different notions have never been defined with much precision, and reportedly aggression was included on the Soviet Union's insistence as marking something even more serious than a breach of the peace. See B.V.A. Röling and Antonio Cassese, *The Tokyo Trial and Beyond* (1993), 101. For a general discussion, see Jan Klabbers, "Intervention, Armed Intervention, Armed

example order that diplomatic relations with the offending state are severed, or order other forms of sanctions, such as a cultural boycott, a sporting boycott or a travel embargo. During the 1990s, it saw fit to set up two criminal tribunals in response to a "Chapter VII situation": the ICTY and the ICTR.[119] And the Security Council can even order or, more commonly, authorize that military troops be sent to the state or region concerned. What the Security Council cannot do, however, is make new international law.

And yet, on occasion it has come perilously close to doing so. A first occasion related to the well-known Lockerbie incident, when the Council imposed sanctions on Libya for failing to hand over two suspected individuals, both of them Libyan nationals. Given the absence of a general duty to extradite suspects in international law, the absence of extradition treaties with the requesting states (the US and the UK), and the fact that it is generally accepted that states need not extradite their own nationals in any circumstances, this can only be seen as an attempt to create new law. This would be a law to the effect that in cases of suspected terrorism, a special extradition rule applies, creating a duty to extradite suspects of terror acts.[120]

The point to note is not that such would be a bad rule, rather it is that the Security Council was never set up as a legislative organ, lacks legislative powers under the Charter of the UN, and is ill-equipped to engage in legislation at any rate. Particularly troublesome is its lack of representativeness: the Council is composed of five permanent members (China, the UK, the US, France and Russia) and ten members that are elected for a period of two years each. Surely, law-making by a club of 15 states in an organization of 193 states is difficult to reconcile with any concept of democracy, and things are even worse upon realizing that Council decisions merely require a majority of nine, including the five permanent members. To leave law-making to a mere 5 per cent of total membership would be undemocratic and highly irresponsible. The Council's somewhat outdated composition is not too much of a

---

Attack, Threat to Peace, Act of Aggression and Threat or Use of Force: What's the Difference?", in Marc Weller (ed.), *The Oxford Handbook on the Use of Force in International Law*, 488–506.

119 International Criminal Tribunal for the former Yugoslavia, and International Criminal Tribunal for Rwanda, respectively.

120 The Court neither confirmed nor denied the proposition when Libya requested provisional measures to protect its rights under international law: see *Case Concerning Questions of Interpretation and Application of the 1971 Montreal Convention arising from the Aerial Incident at Lockerbie* (*Libya* v. *United Kingdom*), order, [1992] ICJ Reports 3.

problem as long as the Council sticks to administrative tasks (although here too it is awkward, in that the permanent five all too rapidly exclude themselves and their client states from enforcement action), but is deeply problematic when it comes to law-making activities.[121]

Still, this has not stopped the Council from further quasi-legislative activities. Two examples have assumed great prominence. Resolution 1373, adopted less than three weeks after the destruction of the twin towers in New York on 11 September 2001, obliges all states to adhere to a number of conventions relating to the financing or suppression of terrorism. Whereas traditionally such conventions would only become binding for the states that ratified them, under Resolution 1373 they also acquired binding force for other states. Since Security Council decisions are binding (by virtue of article 25 of the Charter[122]), it follows that those conventions have acquired binding force through inclusion by the Council. Hence, the Council can be said to have made new anti-terrorism law, despite reservations about the non-existence of legislative powers. Much the same applies to Resolution 1540, aiming to prevent weapons of mass destruction falling into the wrong hands. This resolution, adopted in 2004, orders all states to adopt legislative and enforcement measures to this end, and therewith effectively creates new international law.[123]

In its administrative capacity, the Council has also attracted a considerable amount of flak over the imposition of sanctions, in particular sanctions on individuals. It is undisputed that the Council can subject individuals who are suspected of nefarious activities to individual sanctions. Thus, it can order that bank accounts or other assets be frozen, or that individuals be prevented from travelling. The question that arises though is whether the Council needs in any way to respect the rights of those individuals under the most elementary human rights standards. Thus, if freezing assets is considered a punishment (as it probably should be), then it would seem that a fair trial is called for, and that individuals should have the possibility to appeal.[124] Yet, no mechanisms to this effect exist before the Council, although in

---

121 See Jan Klabbers, "Reflections on the Politics of Institutional Reform", in Peter Danchin and Horst Fischer (eds.), *United Nations Reform and the New Collective Security* (2010), 76–93.

122 They even assume priority over any conflicting obligations under international law by virtue of article 103 UN. For a fine discussion, see Rain Liivoja, "The Scope of the Supremacy Clause of the United Nations Charter", (2008) 57 *International and Comparative Law Quarterly* 583–612.

123 For balanced discussion, see Johnstone, *The Power of Deliberation*.

124 The seminal study is Farrall, *United Nations Sanctions*.

recent years, following highly critical coverage by, in particular, local courts,[125] the Council has given its sanctions-mechanisms a somewhat friendlier face by appointing an ombudsperson to address complaints by targeted individuals.

4.4   Household matters

Even if an organization has no ambition whatsoever to interfere in the affairs of its member states by means of setting standards, its very existence nonetheless entails that a number of decisions must be taken. The organization will have to decide on the appointment of high officials and recruitment of staff generally; it will have to decide on which other states (if any) may join, and perhaps most relevant for all practical purposes, it will have to decide on the budget. Typically, unless the organization is very small, such decisions are taken by majority vote: to insist on unanimity is likely to mean that no budget will ever be adopted, and no leader ever appointed. And typically, since these are matters that can be prepared well in advance, that come back with regularity, and affect the entire membership, they are dealt with by the plenary organ. It is usually the case that the plenary organ, in which all member states sit together, will decide on the appointment of officials, on issues of admission and expulsion, and on the budget.

In the UN, accordingly, these matters are left to the General Assembly, although a certain role is envisaged for the Security Council as well. As discussed above, the Charter envisages an institutional balance between the two organs when it comes to admission of new members: decision by the Assembly upon recommendation by the Council. The same applies, under article 97 of the UN Charter, to the appointment of a new Secretary-General: the decision is to be made by the Assembly on recommendation by the Council. This makes some sense: practically speaking, the Secretary-General needs to have a good working relationship with the five permanent members of the Security Council. Without a decent working relationship, the Secretary-General cannot function properly, as former Secretary-General Boutros Boutros Ghali found out the hard way.[126]

---

125 Of particular relevance is the decision by the CJEU in Case C-402/05 P, *Kadi* v. *Council and Commission* [2008] ECR I-6351.

126 For a useful volume, see Simon Chesterman (ed.), *Secretary or General? The UN Secretary-General in World Politics* (2007).

In the UN, the budgetary power also rests with the General Assembly, and this provides the Assembly with a considerable power basis vis-à-vis the Security Council. After all, it means that whenever the Security Council wants to engage in activities which have financial implications, it can only do so if the Assembly agrees to make the resources available. A celebrated instance hereof occurred when the Council, in controversial circumstances, set up the ICTY in order to prosecute individuals suspected of war crimes and other atrocities in Yugoslavia during the early 1990s. The Assembly was not fully convinced of the wisdom thereof, with some member states fearing that the prosecution of suspects during an ongoing conflict might hamper the prospects for peace. Consequently, the Assembly initially made only limited funding available. Intriguingly, some of the more reluctant states included France and the UK. As these are permanent members of the Security Council, they could have vetoed the creation of the ICTY, but instead chose to operate within the General Assembly.[127] They must have felt that issuing a veto would harm their reputation, and thus found other ways to influence events.

4.5   Recommendations

Around the turn of the twentieth century, two peace conferences were organized in The Hague, in 1899 and 1907. These turned out to be fertile soil for the development of the law of international organizations. Not only were these amongst the first conferences with universal participation, they also experimented with a new type of legal instrument: the states assembled in The Hague would adopt so-called "*voeux*", a French word signifying something like "wish" or "desire". There was an understanding that states would not become legally bound by these *voeux*, but would treat them as recommendations.

Many organizations nowadays use the instrument of the recommendation to signify a course of action deemed desirable. Typically, recommendations are directed at the organization's entire membership, but can be adopted by majority vote. In this way, they manage to reconcile the demands of international cooperation without giving up considerations of state sovereignty: since these recommenda-

---

127   The story of the ICTY's creation is vividly told in Gary J. Bass, *Stay the Hand of Vengeance: The Politics of War Crimes Tribunals* (2000).

tions are not binding, no state will be bound against its will, and yet the organization can claim to have done something about topic X, Y or Z.[128]

The most celebrated examples of recommendations stem from the UN, and amongst these the best-known is the Universal Declaration of Human Rights, adopted as a recommendation by the Assembly (which lacks legislative powers) in 1948. Still, its non-binding origin notwithstanding, the Universal Declaration has proved to be enormously influential. It helped inspire the drafters of the ECHR and other regional human rights treaties; it helped inspire the UN itself to sponsor two broad human rights conventions; and it helped inspire many states to provide for human rights guarantees in their domestic legislation. Many have held that even if the Declaration itself, qua instrument, remains non-binding, most of its contents have acquired binding force through the process of customary international law formation.[129]

Since the standard-setting activities of international organizations have to navigate the rocky shoals between international necessity and member state preference, it is perhaps no coincidence that issuing recommendations has become the default setting of many international organizations, precisely because recommendations can be adopted by majority and do not technically bind anyone to a specific course of action.[130] The drawback is that recommendations are often regarded as somewhat less than full instruments, to be taken less seriously than formally binding instruments. This dissatisfaction has in turn urged some observers to try and upgrade their status, in particular if the recommendations stem from the General Assembly.[131] After all, so the reasoning goes, the General Assembly is the closest thing the world has to a world parliament – should it not follow, therefore, that

---

128 The classic analysis is A.J.P. Tammes, "Decisions of International Organs as a Source of International Law", (1958/II) *Recueil des Cours* 265–363.

129 In a nutshell, customary international law arises if many states engage in similar behaviour and come to accept this behaviour as legally warranted. Thus, if states generally refrain from committing torture, and hold torture to be legally prohibited, one may conclude that the torture prohibition is part of customary international law, and binds even states that have not accepted the prohibition in treaty form. For further discussion, see Jan Klabbers, *International Law* (2013), 26–34.

130 Except, perhaps, to consider it in good faith.

131 Classic studies include Jorge Castaneda, *Legal Effects of United Nations Resolutions* (1969) and Obed Y. Asamoah, *The Legal Significance of the Declarations of the General Assembly of the United Nations* (1966).

recommendations from the Assembly be given more than merely recommendatory force?[132]

The argument may be approached with sympathy, but is difficult to reconcile with the UN Charter. At the end of the day, the Charter does not give the Assembly any legislative powers – had it done so, it is plausible to suspect that some recommendations would never have been adopted: states may with greater ease vote in favour of a recommendation than in favour of a binding instrument. The argument also fails to convince as a matter of democratic theory, if only because not all parliaments have law-making powers. So even if the analogy were correct (which is doubtful: the Assembly represents all member states on the basis of "one state, one vote", and can thus only be considered as a representative organ in a limited sense), the conclusion that therefore the Assembly should be seen as a law-making body does not necessarily follow.

Be that as it may, the UN is not the only international organization gregariously producing recommendations. Many organizations do so, including such august bodies as the ILO, and even the EU, despite its broad law-making powers, sometimes adopts instruments that are, technically, to be considered as non-legally binding. It does so under a wide variety of headings, ranging from Code of Conduct to Guideline. Despite their non-legally binding nature, nonetheless the CJEU has not been shy to grant them some normative effect, for example, as aid to the interpretation of domestic legislation.[133] In other words, the line between legally binding and legally non-binding is, in practice, often difficult to draw, or, more accurately perhaps, not considered to be all that relevant as far as compliance or effectiveness is concerned. States do not adhere to norms solely because these norms are considered "hard" law; instead, states often adhere to norms because they feel doing so is appropriate or to their advantage.

---

132 Perhaps its most prominent proponent was T.O. Elias, a one-time President of the ICJ. See T.O. Elias, "Modern Sources of International Law", in Wolfgang Friedmann et al. (eds.), *Transnational Law in a Changing Society: Essays in Honor of Philip C. Jessup* (1972), 34–69. It is no coincidence, incidentally, that the UN itself is sometimes also regarded as representing the world: see the lively study by Paul Kennedy, *The Parliament of Man: The Past, Present, and Future of the United Nations* (2006).

133 See for example, Jan Klabbers, "International Courts and Informal International Law", in Joost Pauwelyn, Ramses A. Wessel and Jan Wouters (eds.), *Informal International Lawmaking* (2012), 219–40.

Where the distinction does assume relevance, however, is in terms of democratic and judicial overview. It is often the case that non-binding instruments can be adopted without following the prescribed procedure for binding instruments. Thus, within the EU, Guidelines or Codes of Conduct can emanate from the Commission without control by the European Parliament (EP) or the parliaments of the member states. This is less of a problem with other organizations, where recommendations typically stem from the plenary body in which all member states are represented, but even here prescribed procedure may on occasion have to take the backseat.

Some organizations, finally, specialize in the drafting of model legislation or model treaties. These are not in themselves legally binding, but serve as a model for states engaged in relations with each other. A fine example is the model treaty emanating from the OECD on double taxation: many states have mimicked the provisions thereof in their own treaties on double taxation.[134]

4.6 Sponsoring conventions

International organizations function not merely as agents for action, they also serve as platforms for discussion and deliberation. Therewith, they are a well-placed venue for the negotiation of international conventions, especially if those conventions demand the sort of expertise that is present within the organization's bureaucracy. Hence, many organizations tend to be involved in the conclusion of treaties between their member states (and possibly third parties as well).

There is, additionally, a legal factor entering this equation: when organizations first started to take decisions, it was often the case that the precise legal effects of decisions taken by a plenary organ were not spelled out in the constitution. Thus, the effect of such decisions had to be assessed on the spot, and an explanation had to found as to why such decisions could sometimes be regarded as legally binding. The PCIJ found such an explanation in 1931 in what has been called the "treaty analogy". In a dispute between Poland and Lithuania, it held that a decision taken by the Council of the League of Nations was binding because both parties had been participating in its drafting and

---

134 On the OECD's role in standard-setting generally, see Hervé Ascensio and Nicola Bonucci (eds.), *Le pouvoir normatif de l'OCDE* (2013).

could thus be seen as having consented to the decision.[135] In much the same way as treaties are based on the consent of the participating states, here the Court found the decision to be based on state consent, and therewith binding.

The treaty analogy proved helpful when it came to explaining decisions adopted by unanimity or with the active participation of the parties concerned, but proved less helpful to explain majority decisions. Hence, organizations could not turn en masse to taking binding majority decisions – instead, treaty-making remained a favoured technique for law-making. In this context, the organization provides, as it were, the bureaucratic support and the setting, but whether or not states will become bound remains dependent on whether states express their consent to be bound.

The technique of sponsoring conventions is engaged in a great number of organizations. Some use it sparingly: the WHO, for example, has the facility (article 19 WHO Constitution), but has only sponsored one convention. Apparently, its then Director-General was keen to leave a tangible legacy behind, and strongly supported the conclusion of the WHO Framework Convention on Tobacco Control.[136]

In other organizations, however, sponsoring conventions is the organization's bread and butter. The ILO, for example, has sponsored the adoption of some 200 conventions, and has developed specific techniques to make them work. Typically, an ILO convention can enter into force upon having been ratified by a very small number of states (as few as two or three): this exerts some pressure on other states to follow. Moreover, states are expected regularly to explain their failure of ratification (again exercising pressure to join the treaty), and ILO Conventions typically require a very long period of notice if states want to withdraw – sometimes as long as ten years. This discourages withdrawals that take place in the heat of the moment, and gives the withdrawing state ample time to reconsider. It affects the cost-benefit analysis states may make when they realize that withdrawal will only take effect after ten years. Consequently, the ILO has created an

---

135 See *Railway Traffic between Lithuania and Poland* (*Railway Sector Landwarów-Kaisiadorys*), [1931] Publ. PCIJ, Series A/B, no 42. See for further discussion Jan Klabbers, *An Introduction to International Organizations Law* (3rd edn. forthcoming), 158–63.

136 See Gregory F. Jacob, "Without Reservation", (2004) 5 *Chicago Journal of International Law* 287–302.

impressive legal regime, and it is no exaggeration to state that the ILO's existence has made a serious difference: without the organizational backdrop and support, the international labour regime would be far less comprehensive. Without such a backdrop, states would not readily agree, for example, to ten-year periods of notice, or to entry into force upon three ratifications. While it is surely arguable that the ILO has failed to keep up with recent developments, nonetheless it has proved to be quite entrepreneurial.[137]

The former GATT used to sponsor, at first, tariff negotiations between its members: these would bilaterally reduce tariffs in large negotiating rounds. Once tariffs had largely been dismantled (and replaced by other barriers to trade), GATT organized negotiations to dismantle those other barriers to trade, again often on a bilateral basis or between smaller groups of states. Its replacement, the WTO, is considerably less successful, perhaps because thus far it insists on collective change between all its 160 member states: the Doha round of trade negotiations, which commenced in 2001, has yet to be concluded.

The UN also sponsors conventions. Famously, the Genocide Convention of 1948 and the two human rights covenants of 1966 were all negotiated under auspices of the UN. The UN also takes it on itself to help codify and develop international law, and has to this end set up an ILC which, over the years, has played an important role in drafting instruments such as the VCLT or, more recently, the articles on state responsibility.[138]

Even within the EU, its strong legislative powers notwithstanding, the members sometimes conclude treaties on topics related to EU law. Sometimes they do so in smaller groups so as to pioneer particular political projects. An example is the Euro-zone, based on an agreement between some but not all member states to work with a single currency.[139] Sometimes this form of cooperation is meant to complement EU law: over the years, the member states have concluded several treaties on such things as recognition of local judgments. And sometimes, no doubt, it is also meant to circumvent EU law. Since making

---

137 See Jan Klabbers, "Marginalized International Organizations: Three Hypotheses Concerning the ILO", in Ulla Liukkunen and Chen Yifeng (eds.), *China and ILO Fundamental Principles and Rights at Work* (2014), 181–196.

138 These will be further discussed in Chapter 6 below.

139 See generally Filip Tuytschaever, *Differentiation in European Union Law* (1999).

EU legislation often entails an initiating role for the Commission and a controlling role for the EP, it may sometimes be an attractive option for the member states to by-pass the EU altogether and simply conclude an agreement amongst themselves, in particular if they suspect that the Commission or the EP may have objections.

5 Organs and their decisions

5.1 Introduction

Earlier it was suggested that organizations are often set up on the model of a principal–agent relationship. States collectively create an entity to which they then assign a specific function. However, what makes this a curious kind of principal–agent relationship is the circumstance that the principal always makes sure to be part of the agent. All organizations have a plenary body in which the member states are represented. Usually this body meets regularly but not very often (once a year, once every two years). It will discuss the bigger political issues, and will take decisions relating to household matters and issue recommendations that have been negotiated, to a greater or lesser extent, in advance.

Organizations typically also have an administrative organ: a secretariat, however named, to take care of practical matters. Documents need to be typed up and translated, plane tickets and hotels need to be booked, interpreters need to be arranged, and so on: all these matters normally belong to the tasks of the secretariat. On paper, this looks innocent enough, but often the tasks go further as well: meetings of the organization need to be prepared; the agenda needs to be established; and the budget needs to be prepared. Often enough these tasks also fall to the administration, and it is easy to see that here the secretariat has ample space for exercising influence. The task of setting the agenda, for example, entails deciding on what topics are suitable for discussion and what topics should be cast aside, and this, if anything, is the exercise of power.[140] Here then, the *"volonté distincte"* of the organization starts to present itself: the organization, through its administrative organ, not only executes tasks set by the member states, but at the very least helps to shape those tasks and helps to select amongst those tasks. It is no coincidence that social scientists have found that administrative

---

140   See generally the classic study by Steven Lukes, *Power: A Radical View* (1974).

bodies can be powerful actors in their own right. It has been suggested that the inaction of the UN during the genocide in Rwanda in 1994 was mainly due to inertia on the part of the UN bureaucracy.[141]

Since administrative bodies are, in theory at any rate, meant to offer merely secretarial support, and plenary bodies cannot meet on an everyday basis, many organizations have also created an executive organ, tasked with executing the decisions taken by the plenary and preparing the general course of action of the organization. The best-known example is the EU Commission, but the UN Security Council to some extent can also be seen in this light. In some organizations membership of plenary and executive coincide. This is the case in the WTO, for example, which, perhaps for this reason, proudly proclaims itself to be "member-driven". Typically, however, executive bodies are composed of a smaller number of individuals, usually representing their states through some kind of rotating mechanism, sometimes also (as in World Bank and the IMF) representing groups of states, and sometimes even sitting more or less on an individual basis. This latter comment applies mostly to the EU Commission, although even here it is the case that each member state has its own commissioner. Attempts to reduce the number of commissioners have so far not been successful – member states are reluctant to give up their own contact point.

Finally, some organizations have additional institutions in the form of courts or parliaments, but this is rare. The EU has both a court (three courts, in fact[142]) and a parliament, but is unique in this respect. The WTO has a sophisticated legal system in the form of panels and an Appellate Body, but those serve mainly to interpret and apply international trade law: they play little or no constitutional role. If some observers claim that the WTO is basically a trading regime with a judicial system attached, they are hardly distorting the truth.

The UN has something of a court, in the sense that the ICJ is considered one of the principal organs of the UN and has the jurisdiction to deliver advisory opinions on request of other UN organs or certain other organizations associated with the UN.[143] Unlike the EU Court,

---

141   See Michael Barnett and Martha Finnemore, *Rules for the World: International Organizations in Global Politics* (2004).

142   The CJEU and General Court deal with different types of actions, with the CJEU also serving as appellate court. Staff cases are decided by the Civil Service Tribunal.

143   See article 96 of the UN Charter. The leading study is still Kenneth J. Keith, *The Extent of the Advisory Jurisdiction of the International Court of Justice* (1971).

however, the ICJ has been reluctant to assume the power of judicial review over acts of other UN organs. It has sometimes interpreted such legal acts or approved of them, but has never explicitly embraced the power of judicial review, quite possibly because it might fear that in particular the Security Council would not accept being submitted to higher legal authority.[144]

And then some organizations, in particular the EU (not surprisingly given its grand legislative ambitions) are surrounded by hosts of advisory bodies and "watchdog" committees, so much so that the term "comitology" to describe this phenomenon has become a generally accepted and understood phrase. In recent years, moreover, the EU has delegated some of its regulative activities to agencies which, while more or less autonomous, play an important role in creating and managing EU law.[145] The EU also has a parliamentary organ that often acts as formal co-legislator in the form of the EP, and often opens space for discussions with other interested "stakeholders" prior to legislating.

5.2   Creating subsidiary organs

Usually organizations will, at the time of their creation, already have their organs spelled out in their constitutions. Nonetheless, there may always arise a need to create additional organs or, more likely, suborgans. Often, therefore, the constituent documents of organizations will contain some sort of provision on the creation of such subsidiary organs. Surprisingly perhaps, however, those provisions are not always utilized.

The UN Charter contains a number of "regular" provisions on the creation of subsidiary organs. Article 7 provides a general grant to the organization at large to create such subsidiary organs "as may be found necessary". The grant is not a terribly precise one: it does not specify who can create subsidiary organs, nor does it say anything about the procedure to be followed. It also fails to specify which actor or set of actors should find it necessary to create a particular subsidiary organ.

---

144 See Jan Klabbers, "Straddling Law and Politics: Judicial Review in International Law", in R.St.J. MacDonald and D.M. Johnston (eds.), *Towards World Constitutionalism* (2005), 809–35.

145 A very useful discussion is Deirdre Curtin, *Executive Power of the European Union: Law, Practices, and the Living Constitution* (2009).

The other two provisions are drafted a bit more carefully or are, more accurately perhaps, more firmly embedded in a particular legal framework. Article 22 provides that the General Assembly may create "such subsidiary organs as it deems necessary for the performance of its functions", and article 29 uses identical wording to allow the Security Council to do the same thing. Here, then, it is clear who gets to decide, and given the absence of further procedural details, the presumption is that both the Assembly and the Council create such organs via their regular decision-making procedures. With the Assembly that means a two-thirds majority; with the Council it signifies a qualified majority vote, and no vote against by one of the five permanent members. Article 68, finally, allows the Economic and Social Council to set up "commissions", and specifies that some of these shall address economic and social issues and human rights. For example, the much-maligned Human Rights Commission, the predecessor to today's Human Rights Council, was created on this basis.[146]

In addition to these anticipated organs, the Security Council broke relatively new ground[147] when, in the early 1990s, it created two judicial organs on the basis not of article 7 (the general grant) or article 29 (the Council's specific grant), but rather on the basis of Chapter VII of the Charter, as part of the UN's involvement in restoring peace and security. Clearly, to establish such a tribunal on the basis of a regular treaty to be negotiated between the member states would be too lengthy a process, and would not guarantee that Yugoslavia and its successor states would become parties – so the regular treaty basis was not deemed fruitful.

Surprisingly, however, article 29 was not considered to be an option either; in fact, it was not even considered.[148] The reason for bypassing article 29 must have been the pragmatic one that action under Chapter VII carries a degree of seriousness which is not attached to other Security Council action. Technically, a decision under article 29 would be just as binding as a decision under Chapter VII, but since Chapter VII is typically used in matters of crisis and urgency, its use sends a message. While it has also been suggested that article 29 does

---

146 See generally Klabbers, "Reflections on the Politics of Institutional Reform".

147 In the aftermath of the 1991 Gulf War, the Council had established several bodies on the basis of Chapter VII, including a boundary demarcation commission and a commission to decide on claims for compensation by those who had suffered damage.

148 The relevant UN Doc is S/25704, in which the Secretary-General proposed how to set up the ICTY. It only mentions article 29 in passing.

not allow for subsidiary organs to take binding decisions, if so, the textual basis for this requirement is unclear. There is nothing in the text of article 29 that suggests as much.[149]

Either way, in the well-known *Tadic* case, the ICTY's Appeals Chamber was asked to rule on the legality of the creation of the ICTY, and found no problem with it. According to the Appeals Chamber, article 41 of the UN Charter provides the Security Council with an almost unfettered discretion to take whatever kind of measure it feels is necessary to restore or maintain international peace and security. And if the Council feels that establishing war crimes tribunals is necessary for the restoration or maintenance of peace and security, then so be it: the Charter places no limits on the Council's power to take measures under article 41, other, perhaps, than the injunction against using forcible measures – these can be taken under article 42, but cannot be justified under article 41.[150]

The legality of the creation of subsidiary organs has also come before the ICJ. An advisory opinion issued in 1954 addressed the creation of an Administrative Tribunal of the UN (UNAT) by the General Assembly. UNAT had been created in order to settle labour-related disputes between the UN and its staff. The ICJ suggested that the Assembly's power to create a judicial organ capable of issuing binding financial decisions derived not so much from articles 7 or 22 of the UN Charter, but could rather be justified on the basis of an implied power: setting up UNAT "was essential to ensure the efficient working of the Secretariat, and to give effect to the paramount consideration of securing the highest standards of efficiency, competence and integrity".[151] The Court construed the UN Charter to contain an implied power to set up UNAT, and only referred to articles 7 and 22 to illustrate that this particular power could be exercised on behalf of the UN by the Assembly.

---

149 The argument is made by Andreas Paulus, "Article 29", in Bruno Simma et al. (eds.), *The Charter of the United Nations: A Commentary* (3rd edn, 2012), 987–1027. He refers to the decision on interlocutory appeal on jurisdiction of the ICTY Appeals Chamber in *Prosecutor* v. *Dusko Tadic* in support, but the decision does not pay attention to article 29. It is reproduced in 105 ILR 453.

150 Plausible as the reasoning of the Appeals Chamber is, letting part of the ICTY decide on the legality of the creation of the same ICTY means the decision will always be vulnerable to criticism.

151 See *Effect of Awards*, 57.

5.3   Delegation

One of the theoretical puzzles of the law of international organizations concerns the phenomenon of delegation, and the puzzle is manifested in various ways. It is often seen as a general principle that a delegated power cannot be further delegated, the reason being that if delegation were to occur down several levels, control would be difficult to exercise, which in turn would have all kinds of consequences for issues of responsibility. Simply put, if John orders his son to get him a soda from the fridge, the son delegates the task to his sister, who in turn delegates it to a cousin, who in turn delegates it to a friend who happens to be in the same place, then who should John blame (or thank) if instead of a soda, he is eventually brought a beer?

The main problem now arises upon realizing that organizations themselves are often seen as exercising delegated powers.[152] If this is accurate, and if the general principle is accurate, then it follows that organizations cannot themselves engage in further delegations of powers. And yet practice suggests that such delegations are frequent occurrences: the very rationale behind a legal power to create subsidiary organs is precisely to have an appropriate body available to delegate tasks to.

To make things more complicated still, some relationships are best construed as further delegations to (some of the) member states.[153] The classic example concerns the UN setting up peace enforcement missions: member states have delegated that task to the UN, which then further delegates it to some of its member states, namely those who are willing and able to participate. And this raises difficult issues not just about whether such re-delegation is possible or acceptable as a matter of political theory, but also in relation to the source of instruction. Hypothetically, the member states concerned could ignore instructions from the UN by claiming that the UN is merely their creation to begin with.

---

152 International lawyers have not written much on the topic, with the exception of Sarooshi's work. See Dan Sarooshi, *The United Nations and the Development of Collective Security: The Delegation by the UN Security Council of its Chapter VII Powers* (1999), and Dan Sarooshi, *International Organizations and their Exercise of Sovereign Powers* (2005).

153 See Niels M. Blokker, "Is the Authorization Authorized? Powers and Practice of the UN Security Council to Authorize the Use of Force by 'Coalitions of the Willing'", (2000) 11 *European Journal of International Law* 541–68.

There is surprisingly little general case-law on the forms, proprieties and modalities of delegations of power. The leading judicial decision is generally held to be the 1958 *Meroni* case of the CJEU. In 1955, the High Authority of the European Coal and Steel Community (ECSC)[154] had set up a specific agency to decide on issues relating to scrap metal, and in doing so had delegated powers that the ECSC member states had earlier delegated to the High Authority, while leaving the agency a large measure of discretion. The High Authority would accept decisions taken by the agency as binding, without exercising any further control, and without regard to the obligations that would rest on the High Authority if it would exercise the task itself. This meant that the agency in question was given broader powers and more discretion than the High Authority itself possessed and this, so the Court held, was not a good idea: you cannot delegate powers you do not possess yourself.[155]

In the literature, sometimes a distinction is made between a delegation of powers and a transfer of powers. Delegation would, in principle, be temporary, and subject to control by the principal (the delegator), whereas a transfer of powers is considered permanent and no longer subject to control by the principal. The distinction is analytically useful, but in practice the dividing lines tend to be fuzzier than the distinction presupposes. Not only may some kind of control remain to be exercised even after a transfer, it also appears that transferred powers can nonetheless be revoked or, as someone once graphically put it, repatriated.[156]

5.4   The international civil service

Like all bureaucracies, international organizations need people to make them work. In the early days of international organizations, those people were often supplied by the host state, were nationals of the host state, and were on the payroll of the host state. But with the creation of the League of Nations, this practice slowly came

---

154 The High Authority was the predecessor of what is today referred to as the EU Commission, in other words, the executive organ of the ECSC.

155 See Case 9/56, *Meroni and others* v. *High Authority*, [1958] ECR 133. The case was still relied on by the CJEU in Case C-270/12, *United Kingdom* v. *European Parliament and Council*, judgment of 22 January 2014, nyr, relating to the creation of the European Securities and Markets Authority (ESMA).

156 See Daniela Obradovic, "Repatriation of Powers in the European Community", (1997) 34 *Common Market Law Review* 59–88.

to be seen as undesirable: if the organization was supposed to rise beyond any narrow national interest, it required staff members capable of transcending their own national backgrounds. To that end, the League's director at the time, Sir Eric Drummond, stimulated the creation of an international civil service, composed of individuals with a cosmopolitan, internationalist outlook. And this outlook was to be nurtured by special educational institutions, such as the Graduate Institute of International and Development Studies in Geneva, created in 1927.

Many constituent documents have come to contain a provision regarding the neutrality or impartiality of staff. Article 100 UN Charter, for example, provides that staff members shall not seek any instructions from any authority external to the UN, and that member states shall respect the international character of the tasks of UN staff and shall "not seek to influence them in the discharge of their responsibilities". While the rule may often be "honoured in the breach", as international lawyers are wont to put it euphemistically, nonetheless articles such as these hold that the staff is supposed to represent the "view from nowhere": such articles assume that there is an international position possible which cannot be identified with any member state or group of member states, but it is doubtful whether this is a realistic assumption.

In most organizations, staff will be hired in a trade-off between individual qualifications and political realities: organizations need to hire competent staff, but also need to make sure that different regions are adequately represented. It is easy to dismiss the latter as silly politics, but such would be a bit unfair: the organization derives part of its elusive legitimacy from how its staff is composed. Put graphically, if the United Nations Development Programme (UNDP) were to be staffed solely by middle-aged white men, it would not get much done in many of the countries where it is active, no matter how technically competent those middle-aged white men might be.

Indeed, the composition of staff can be influential in unexpected ways which have little to do with evil intentions. Anthropological work suggests strongly that one of the reasons why the World Bank is not too keen on adopting human rights as a framework for its activities resides in the circumstance that the Bank's staff is predominantly composed of economists. Economists are professionally trained to think in terms of costs and benefits, rather than rights and obligations – hence, the mindset of many Bank employees is simply not geared towards think-ing in terms of human rights.[157]

Amongst staff members, the Director-General or Secretary-General (SG) occupies a special position. He (the number of women leading an international organization is still embarrassingly small) is both staff member and policy-maker, both servant and master of the organization. Under article 99 of the UN Charter, the Secretary-General can bring matters to the attention of the Security Council. This suggests that he is expected to play a role in global politics and, indeed, some incumbents have been very active, none more so perhaps than Dag Hammarskjöld.[158] Yet, on the other hand, the Secretary-General is but a servant of the organization, and at the very least needs to make sure to have a decent working relationship with powerful member states. And this calls for a delicate balancing act on the part of the individual concerned.[159]

As already alluded to, the international civil service cannot usually rely on the protection of national courts in labour disputes: organizations will quickly invoke immunity from suit. This can sometimes lead to injustice. A famous case, for example, was brought in the late 1970s – in vain – before a US court by a World Bank employee, Susanna Mendaro, who felt she had been subjected to harassment and discrimi-nation by her superiors. In order to fill the void, many organizations have created their own administrative tribunal, or have accepted the jurisdiction of the ILOAT so as to provide a remedy in case of staff dis-putes. The EU has had its own Civil Service Tribunal since 2005; earlier cases were brought to the CJEU or the former Court of First Instance, now known as the General Court. The UN streamlined its system in 2009, and now has a two-tier process with a Dispute Tribunal and an Appeals Tribunal. Its earlier mechanism, the UN Administrative Tribunal, discussed earlier, was no longer considered to be up to the demands of modern conceptions of justice.[160]

---

157 See the excellent study by Galit A. Sarfaty, *Values in Translation: Human Rights and the Culture of the World Bank* (2012).

158 See generally the fine study by Manuel Fröhlich, *Political Ethics and the United Nations: Dag Hammarskjöld as Secretary-General* (2008). Hammarskjöld was killed in mysterious circum-stances in a plane crash, giving rise to many a conspiracy theory. For a discussion of some of these, see Susan Williams, *Who Killed Hammarskjöld? The UN, the Cold War and White Supremacy in Africa* (2013).

159 Kofi Annan quipped, not unreasonably, that SG stands for "scapegoat". See Kofi Annan with Nader Mousavizadeh, *Interventions: A Life in War and Peace* (2012), 139.

160 See above, Chapter 2, section 2.5.

5.5   Towards secondary law?

When the US (and the UK) planned to invade Iraq in 2003, several arguments were presented to justify the invasion. Some related to the law on the use of force: the action was presented as an exercise in self-defence, however preemptive perhaps. Some related to general political concerns: the world needed to be made safe from a dictator (Saddam Hussein) who, moreover, supposedly had close ties to the terrorists of Al-Qaida. And one of the arguments referred back to action taken against Iraq a decade earlier, after it had invaded Kuwait. In the early 1990s, the UN had responded by sending a military mission and, when the operation proved successful, imposed surrender upon Iraq with a number of conditions. The reasoning then in 2003 was that these resolutions of 1991 were still active: since Hussein was thought to have been in breach of the resolutions, therefore, an invasion was nothing more than enforcement of those earlier resolutions.

Whether this was plausible or not,[161] the argument exploited the circumstance that the relevant resolutions were not embedded in any legal regime relating to the legal validity of decisions of international organizations and their organs. There exist rules on the proper procedure to be followed when it comes to the adoption of decisions – each organization has its own rules, and its own procedures. But there are few, if any, rules on how decisions are to be terminated, or on their geographical reach. The relevant 1991 resolutions had remained silent, and thus, absent any general rules, the argument that they were still in force may not have been the most plausible, but was not completely eccentric either.

To some extent, some general rules are in the process of being developed or recognized. Starting from discussions on the accountability of international organizations and borrowing freely from domestic notions of administrative law, there is room for the argument that organizations cannot entirely do as they please anymore. Even so, perhaps precisely because their origins lie in discussions on accountability, such conceptions tend to have greater traction when it comes to assessing whether the application of international law is done properly than in evaluating whether the contents of that law is itself proper.[162]

---

161   A forceful critique can be found in A.V. Lowe, *International Law* (2007).

162   This refers to the global administrative law project in particular. See Benedict Kingsbury, Nico Krisch and Richard Stewart, "The Emergence of Global Administrative Law", (2005) 68 *Law and Contemporary Problems*, 15–61. See also Eyal Benvenisti, *The Law of Global Governance* (2014).

The discipline, in other words, is in need of some general rules of secondary law, if only to indicate how long organizational decisions that have no dispositive effect remain in force. A decision allowing a state to join an organization is dispositive (unless stated otherwise): it creates a new legal situation, and that situation can only be changed by adopting a new instrument, for example a decision to expel the state concerned. But many decisions are open-ended, and thus need, for example, some time-limits. If the decision itself states to be valid for a certain period of time only, then that will be the case, but if the decision remains silent, then a general default rule could be useful.

What applies to the factor time also applies to the spatial, personal and substantive scope of decisions. In principle, like all legal instruments, organizational decisions have their effects in time, in space, over persons, and over subject matter. Thus, a decision to combat piracy off the Somali coast will need to define where exactly such a mission can operate; whether, for example, it covers only the high seas or also the territorial waters of Somalia. It will also need to define its substantive scope: what does it mean by piracy? To some extent, spatial and substantive scope go hand in hand here: since piracy is generally considered as limited to acts taking place on the high seas, a decision on piracy is limited in application to the high seas, unless further specifications are made. To some extent, however, a separate indication of the substantive scope may still be required: since piracy requires the involvement of two ships, acts taking place on board a single ship (robbery, for example) are not captured by the notion of piracy and thus need to be specifically mentioned. The example illustrates the complexities involved in drafting resolutions. Many of these complexities will remain, but some might be taken care of by general default rules of secondary law.

Even the preliminary question of what exactly constitutes a decision of an organization may be subjected to some default rule or other. Thus, since the Security Council generally meets at the ambassadorial level, it stands to reason to treat decisions taken by the assembled ambassadors as Security Council resolutions. Sometimes, however, the Council meets at the level of Heads of State and Government: these form special summit meetings of the Council. Then the question arises whether decisions adopted at such a meeting are best seen as Security Council decisions, or as agreements between the 15 participating states. The difference can be consequential: if the former is the case, the decision is binding on all members of the UN. If, by contrast, it is better seen as an agreement between the 15 members of the Council, then it can only bind those 15 states. In such a context, much is to be said for the creation of a secondary set of rules to settle such questions, or at least to establish a default position.[163]

To some extent, organizations themselves are moving in this direction. Organizations such as the World Bank and IMF have adopted internal guidelines and policy directives, and many Security Council resolutions nowadays are specific in their use of details and contain a clause on their duration. Still, since there are at least 300 organizations in existence, if all are to develop their own rules, the result will be a highly fragmented regime. Then again, in such a fragmented landscape, the development of general rules might simply not be possible.

---

163 The point is inspired by Feichtner, *The Law and Politics of WTO Waivers*, esp. 163–69.

6   Accountability

6.1   Introduction

International organizations, as has been mentioned before, have always been conceptualized as functional entities, set up by member states to perform specific functions, and ultimately subject to control by those same member states. They are given specific powers, and those powers form the limits of what they were supposed to do. Should an organization overstep the boundaries of its powers (act ultra vires), the decision or act concerned should be considered invalid.

This conception was happily embraced in theory, but its practical application received a considerable blow in the ICJ's 1962 advisory opinion in *Certain Expenses*.[164] At issue was peacekeeping by the UN upon recommendation by the General Assembly. Since this was not provided for in the Charter (which had only envisaged military action ordered or authorized by the Security Council), some important member states objected to having to pay for what they held to constitute ultra vires activities. The Court disagreed, and made two important claims. First, it felt that even if an activity were beyond the powers of a particular organ, it could still be within the powers of the organization at large. In other words, even if the General Assembly had overstepped its powers, this did not automatically mean that therewith the act was ultra vires – it might still be within the powers of the UN, as long as the UN could make plausible that a link existed between the act and the UN's broader functions. If so, "the presumption is that such action is not *ultra vires* the Organization".[165] Second, the Court opined that inevitably, given the absence of regular judicial review procedures, each organ must decide for itself on the proper scope of its competences, at least at first sight.[166] If all organs are the judges of their

---

164 See also above, Chapter 3 section 3.3.
165 See *Certain Expenses*, 168.
166 *Ibid.*

own activities, and acts are not easily to be presumed as ultra vires, it follows that the mechanisms by which member states can control their organizations are limited indeed.

Mostly, then, these mechanisms consist of blunt political instruments: member states can decide to withhold their compulsory contributions if they think the organization is doing something it should not be doing. Alternatively, they can try and replace the organization's management, as happened in the UN after Boutros Ghali lost the confidence of the US government and was replaced by Kofi Annan,[167] or as happened when the Director-General of the Organization for the Prohibition of Chemical Weapons (OPCW) was ousted.[168] Or member states can withdraw from the organization to express their dissatisfaction and prompt the organization to change its ways.[169] All these, however, are blunt instruments, which can (and usually are) also used for reasons unrelated to the functioning of the organization and unrelated to whether it functions in accordance with the limits set by its constituent document.

6.2   Responsibility becomes an issue

Even the idea that the ultra vires doctrine would largely remain ineffective was for a long time not considered to be much of a problem. After all, in the unlikely event that organizations would do something wrong, clearly the member states would be to blame, either for making the organization do wrong, or for failing to prevent the wrong. It is no coincidence then that early attempts to discuss the responsibility of international organizations quickly lapsed into discussions of the responsibility of the member states of the organization.[170]

And yet, by the 1960s organizations had started to lose some of their halo. Local courts were confronted with claims by individuals who had lost property in UN operations, for example, or confronted by claims from disgruntled international civil servants who had been passed over

---

167 Boutros Ghali finished his regular first term, but was prevented, against initial expectations, from serving a second term.

168 See Jan Klabbers, "The *Bustani* Case before the ILOAT: Constitutionalism in Disguise?", (2004) 53 *International and Comparative Law Quarterly* 455–64.

169 As discussed above, in Chapter 3 section 3.4.

170 See, classically, Clyde Eagleton, "International Organization and the Law of Responsibility", (1959/I) 76 *Recueil des Cours* 319–425.

for a promotion, or had not been given the permanent contract they thought they were entitled to. Those local courts could still uphold the immunity of the organization from local jurisdiction, but over time it became clear that the organization would suffer a legitimacy crisis if it would engage in wrongdoing without allowing for some mechanism to hold it accountable. Hence, although administrative tribunals to hear staff disputes had already existed, their number grew, and the UN started to provide for mechanisms to accommodate, for example, the victims of traffic incidents involving the UN as well as for problems that may arise during operational activities.[171]

Things really got out of hand during the 1980s, with the collapse of the International Tin Council. The Tin Council was an international organization based in London and devoted to stabilizing the world market for tin products. In order to do this, it would buy tin if the market price was low (artificially raising demand and therewith the market price), and sell it when it was high again (doing the reverse). This way, tin producers would see their income stabilize, and tin consumers would see their costs stabilize. For this to work, however, borrowing large sums of money was inevitable, and the moment arrived when the Council was no longer capable of paying off its debts. Hence, it became insolvent, and when the underlying international tin agreement expired in 1989, the member states did not take steps to renew it.

The money lenders started legal proceedings in order to retrieve their money, and the question arose whether the member states could be obliged to compensate for the losses incurred by the Tin Council's operations. Various court proceedings took place in various English courts at various levels, all leading to the same result: the Tin Council had been an international organization, complete with a legal personality separate from its member states. It followed that the member states (distinct legal persons, after all), could not be held liable. As some observed, this may entail a grave injustice, but the law allowed for no other solution.

The Tin Council litigation served as the proverbial wake up call for the international legal community, and gave rise to a veritable cottage industry of doctoral theses and attempts to formulate rules on accountability of international organizations. The need for some

---

171 A very useful overview is provided by Kirsten Schmalenbach, *Die Haftung internationaler Organisationen* (2004).

rules became even more visible when, in the 1990s, the UN started to administer territory, first in East Timor, later also in Kosovo. In those territories, the UN organs and other international organizations exercised governmental and policing tasks, which had the ability to affect people's lives in a very real way: one could be arrested and placed in jail by international officials in the name of the international community.[172] In such circumstances, it became clear that the activities of international organizations should somehow be subjected to some kind of control. It would need to be clear what international law rules rest on international organizations; it would need to be clear when international organizations engage in wrongful acts; and it would need to be clear what to do about wrongful acts of organizations.

Already a few years before the Tin Council crisis, but hardly noticed at the time, the ICJ had been confronted with a relevant case, and had been by and large unable to present a credible, principled answer. The situation was this. As early as the nineteenth century, an international health bureau had been established in Alexandria, in Egypt. This functioned independently for many years, and after the Second World War came to be integrated in the newly established WHO. It remained headquartered in Egypt, on the basis of two host agreements, a formal one and a more informal one. When Egypt in 1978 made peace with Israel and even concluded a peace agreement a year later, it became something of an outcast amongst large parts of the Arab world, and a movement gathered pace to relocate the office from Alexandria to Amman, in Jordan. The question arose whether this could be done by the WHO, exercising its powers, or whether somehow the treaty partner would need to have a say in all this. The Court made clear that the treaty partner (in other words, Egypt) could not be ignored: the WHO could not just take a decision and confront Egypt with it. Egypt, in fact, occupied a dual position: it was both inside and outside the WHO; both a member state and a treaty partner. As member state it would be implicated in any decision the WHO would take, but as treaty partner, it could not possibly be bound by any decision taken by the WHO. Hence, a stalemate ensued, which the Court could only resolve by suggesting that the matter be settled by agreement and in good faith along the lines suggested in the VCLT. The upshot is that it became clear that the law of international organizations has no facilities for dealing with issues affecting third parties (such as Egypt, in the case at hand):

---

172   For a brilliant genealogy, see Anne Orford, *International Authority and the Responsibility to Protect* (2011).

control by member states alone might not do the trick unless those member states are seriously willing to protect the interests of third parties. But this is, obviously, not something one can always rely on: in fact, the Egypt example made clear that the member states might not be willing even to protect the interests of one of their own.

The same problem manifested itself when the ILC – a subsidiary organ of the General Assembly of the UN – tried to formulate rules on the law governing treaties concluded with or between international organizations. The question arose whether member states of an organization are bound by treaties concluded by an organization they are members of: if NATO concludes a treaty with, say, Japan, does such a treaty contain obligations for NATO member states such as Belgium, the US or Turkey?

The ILC saw itself confronted by two competing visions. On the one hand, organizations are set up by member states to perform functions for those member states, so it would seem reasonable to hold that those member states incur obligations when their organizations conclude a treaty. Yet, this position would undermine the separate identity (perhaps even legal personality) of the organization in question. On the other hand, however, if the organization is indeed a distinct entity, it follows that member states must be seen as third parties, and under the classic law of treaties, a treaty cannot create rights or obligations for third parties without their consent. This would have the drawback, however, of ignoring the fact that often organizations rely on member states for the implementation of treaty commitments: since NATO has no troops of its own, it needs to rely on member state troops.[173] The special rapporteur appointed by the ILC eventually formulated a compromise, but this did not make it into the final text of what became the 1986 Vienna Convention on the Law of Treaties Concluded with or Between International Organizations, largely because it was considered too cumbersome.[174]

---

173 The general point holds even if member state troops are placed at NATO's permanent disposal – they remain member state troops. Lacking the power to tax, NATO cannot set up troops in isolation from its member states.

174 The 1986 Vienna Convention has yet to enter into force. The debate on the position of member states is authoritatively discussed in Catherine M. Brölmann, "The 1986 Vienna Convention on the Law of Treaties: The History of Draft Article 36*bis*", in Jan Klabbers and René Lefeber (eds.), *Essays on the Law of Treaties: A Collection of Essays in Honour of Bert Vierdag* (1998), 121–40.

6.3 Articles on the Responsibility of International Organizations (ARIO)

In 2000, the same ILC started a long-term project to draft a set of rules on the responsibility of international organizations. It appointed a special rapporteur, Italian law professor (now Judge) Giorgio Gaja, and set about to describe and develop rules on when organizations could be held responsible under international law, and what the consequences of such responsibility would be. This was circumscribed by a number of factors. First, since the ILC was just finishing a long-term project on the responsibility of states, it was felt desirable that the rules on responsibility of international organizations would closely follow the rules on state responsibility. Second, the ILC's work was made more difficult given the scarcity of practice: if the rules on responsibility of states have a long pedigree in international law, with the ILC being able to draw on a century's worth of case-law from international courts, national courts and diplomatic practice, the operations of international organizations had not yet given rise to a lot of practice. Hence, much of the law had to be developed on a hypothetical basis. Third, there is the awkward circumstance that while most states are fairly similar (at least for purposes of international law), international organizations come in many variations, ranging from the almost state-like EU to entities with very specific functions. Some organizations handle large sums of money (think of the financial institutions), others are predominantly vehicles to facilitate a specific task. The landscape, in other words, shows a far greater variety than that of states, which inevitably raises the issue whether a rule that would be appropriate for, say, the World Bank, would also be appropriate for, say, the Office France-Allemand pour la Jeunesse.

The ILC concluded its project in 2011 with the adoption of a set of articles, but the international community's reception has been, at best, somewhat lukewarm. Most observers agree that it is useful that some rules have now been authoritatively formulated, but few have been wildly enthusiastic. International organizations bemoan the lack of underlying practice, and often suggest that even if the rules are fine in general, they are less appropriate for their specific situations.[175]

Perhaps the biggest problem with the ARIO, as the articles have come to be known under their acronym, is that they follow the rules on state

---

175 A useful collection is Maurizio Ragazzi (ed.), *Responsibility of International Organizations: Essays in Memory of Sir Ian Brownlie* (2013).

responsibility too closely although, in fairness to special rapporteur Gaja, it could hardly have been otherwise. The problem then is this. The rules on state responsibility presuppose a fairly classic model of international law, as dealing with a world comprised of states that are all sovereign, and are all of equal legal standing, regardless of power differences. Those states enter into relations with each other, and it makes sense to hold them responsible if and when they do wrong towards each other. While it is also the case that organizations enter into relations with each other and with states, and thus it is sensible to hold them responsible if and when they do wrong, nonetheless the main problem connected to the operations of organizations is when they exercise public power – yet because of the analogy with state responsibility, this dimension is by and large absent from the ARIO. The ARIO provide useful services when UNICEF or the OAS breaches a treaty commitment towards Japan or Uzbekistan or Somalia, but is far less useful when the UN commits a wrong towards someone living in a territory administered by the UN; when UNHCR commits a wrong towards a refugee residing in a refugee camp run by UNHCR; or when the EU wrongly arrests a Somali suspect of piracy. In technical terms, the ARIO, like the articles on state responsibility, are based on a private law paradigm, but that paradigm is of limited use only when the acts of international organizations are at issue. Instead, a public law paradigm would have been more appropriate, but such a paradigm was well-nigh foreclosed by the political imperative of following the model set by the rules on state responsibility.[176]

Be that as it may, the ARIO are built around the concept of the international wrongful act which, in turn, comprises two elements.[177] An internationally wrongful act consists, first, of a breach of an international legal obligation, and second, the breach must be attributable to the organization. Both elements are difficult: it is not immediately self-evident which international legal obligations rest upon international organizations, and since acts of organizations are often performed by individuals who may be part of the national executive, it may not always be easy to tell who did what exactly. By way of (hypothetical, and stark) example, if a Canadian peacekeeper operating in a UN mission in Liberia arbitrarily detains a civilian, the first question to ask is whether the UN is bound under international law not to engage in

---

176 For useful discussion of the various paradigms of responsibility, see Peter Cane, *Responsibility in Law and Morality* (2002).

177 See article 4 ARIO.

arbitrary detention. Second, the question arises whether the act can be attributed to the peacekeeper, the UN, Canada, or to all three.[178]

The first question seems unproblematic but, on reflection, may not be all that easy to answer.[179] The UN is not a party to any human rights convention, and thus not under any treaty-based obligation not to engage in arbitrary detentions. That leaves two other possibilities. First, the UN has sponsored several human rights conventions, including conventions which contain a prohibition of arbitrary detention. In such a case, the argument can be made that since the UN has sponsored such conventions, it would be difficult for the UN to claim that is has nothing to do with them. And, indeed, politically this would be an awkward argument to make. It would raise the critique of double standards (the UN makes rules for others but not for itself), and it would be difficult to comprehend in terms of the UN's mission. Surely, it would be odd if an organization devoted to the pursuit of global justice would extract itself from basic human rights.[180] Note, however, that while politically awkward, as a legal argument it is not fully convincing, in particular as it fails to explain why organizations can be bound merely through the act of sponsoring a convention while states can only be bound after having expressed their consent. Nothing would prevent a state from hosting or sponsoring a convention to conclude a human rights treaty and subsequently not signing or ratifying the treaty, and no one would consider the state in question as legally bound.[181]

A second avenue might hold that the UN is legally bound, under international law, not to engage in arbitrary detention because the prohibition thereof is accepted as part of customary international law, which binds all actors regardless of whether they have explicitly consented. Again, the thought is attractive, but not without problems, as customary law typically reflects the standards prevailing within a

178 There might be additional elements involved still. For instance, responsibility can perhaps also be attributed to the force commander, who may be of different nationality still.

179 There is the additional consideration that sometimes the law itself might be instrumental in justifying great suffering: think for instance of the legal imposition of sanctions. Such a scenario is explored in Scott Veitch, *Law and Irresponsibility: On the Legitimation of Human Suffering* (2007).

180 Reasoning along these lines helped to justify the creation of the UN Administrative Tribunal in the late 1940s, according to the ICJ. See *Effect of Awards*.

181 Not entirely on point, but still illustrative, the League of Nations had been pushed by US President Wilson, yet the US never joined. The history of the Versailles negotiations is well-told in Margaret MacMillan, *Paris 1919: Six Months that Changed the World* (2003).

delimited political community.[182] In international law, that community has traditionally been the community of states; to expand the reach of customary international law to encompass other actors as well might demand a further explanation. In short, the basis of legal obligation is problematic when it comes to international organizations. It may well be the case, as the ICJ suggested in 1980, that organizations are legally bound by the treaties to which they are parties, their internal rules, and the "general rules of international law", but in particular the reach of the latter is unclear, and the ARIO do not provide much by way of elaboration.[183]

If the basis of obligation is problematic, so too are issues of attribution. Here, the ARIO envisage several possibilities. First, the organization will be responsible for the conduct of its own officials and organs (article 6 of the ARIO), but it may also incur responsibility for the conduct of organs or agents of states placed at the organization's disposal, if the organization exercises "effective control" (article 7 of the ARIO). The problem then is to figure out what exactly "effective control" means, and this may differ from situation to situation. Additionally, conduct may be attributed to the organization if the organization "adopts" it (article 9 of the ARIO). Along these lines, the EU habitually adopts customs practices engaged in by its member states and assumes responsibility for these practices.

Things become even more complicated in other situations. Thus, the ARIO hold that organizations may incur responsibility if they assist others in the commission of wrongful acts (article 14 of the ARIO), or if they direct or even coerce others into committing wrongful acts (articles 15 and 16 of the ARIO), or if they order or authorize the commission of wrongful acts by member states (article 17 of the ARIO).

A separate question is whether attribution can only be done to a single actor, or whether the same behaviour can possibly be attributed to several actors simultaneously. In one ill-received decision, the ECtHR assumed that the former was the case: once it found the behaviour of UN and NATO agents in Kosovo during the UN's administration to be attributable to the UN, it declined to look further into the question

---

182   See generally David J. Bederman, *Custom as a Source of Law* (2010).

183   In the literature, sophisticated attempts have been made to hold organizations legally bound by customary international law. See, for example, Guglielmo Verdirame, *The UN and Human Rights: Who Guards the Guardians?* (2011).

whether nonetheless member states of those organizations could also be held responsible.[184] The decision was ill-received because in finding the behaviour attributable to the UN, the Court decided it could not further discuss the case: the UN is not a party to the ECHR, and thus outside the jurisdiction of the ECtHR, and this entailed, so commentators complained, that relief was denied to the victims. Arguably, since the case had been brought against several member states, the Court should have investigated whether simultaneous attribution of conduct to both the UN and the member states in question was a possibility, but it did no such thing.[185]

6.4   Alternative attempts

The ARIO represent a classical, traditional way of establishing a regime related to the responsibility of international organizations: it assumes that actors (organizations, in this case) are bound under international law, that they breach those obligations, and that if the breach is attributable to them, they will be held responsible. As noted before, this may well work, but the circumstances in which it will work are limited, partly for reasons of attribution, partly because of the absence of a public law paradigm, and partly because it remains unclear how and when international organizations become bound by international law.[186]

Several alternative, less traditional, attempts have been formulated over the last two decades in order to underline that organizations cannot just do as they please and conduct their business without any form of control. Three of these may be singled out: the accountability project of the International Law Association (ILA), the Global Administrative Law (GAL) approach, and the putative constitutionalization of international organizations.

During the 1990s, the ILA, a professional organization of international lawyers with several thousands of members worldwide, placed what it

---

184 See joined cases *Behrami and Behrami* v. *France* (application no. 71412/01) and *Saramati* v. *France and others* (application no. 78166/91), decision of 2 May 2007, reproduced in 133 ILR 1.

185 For strong criticism to this effect, see Verdirame, *The UN and Human Rights*.

186 There is some wisdom in suggesting that ARIO's most pronounced effect will be to steer and guide debate about the conduct of international organizations. See Kristina Daugirdas, "Reputation and the Responsibility of International Organizations", (2014) 25 *European Journal of International Law* 991–1018.

referred to as the "accountability" of international organizations on its agenda. With the help of two rapporteurs, professors Malcolm Shaw and Karel Wellens, the ILA's committee on the topic presented several reports over the years, with a final report being adopted in 2004. This final report develops a set of "Recommended Rules and Practices" relating to the behaviour of international organizations, positing that they should respect their internal rules and treaty obligations, but also a number of notions derived from common sense, best practices, "good governance", and the like. One of the reasons for this broad approach, so it was acknowledged, was precisely because of the lack of clarity surrounding the basis of legal obligation for international organizations.[187]

Like the ARIO adopted by the ILC, the recommended rules and practices devised by the ILA have not met with an enthusiastic reception, and it seems fair to say that they are close to having been forgotten. Partly this stems, no doubt, from the considerable level of detail employed by the ILA. Thus, to take one example, not only does the ILA stipulate that organizations and their organs should state the reasons for the decisions they take, they also specify that general decisions should only be based on general reasons, and that decisions affecting particular persons should reflect the particular circumstances underlying the decision. This may be an expression of the regular lawyerly instinct to be as precise and comprehensive as possible in drafting normative instruments, but it comes close to legislative overkill. Moreover, some of the recommended rules and practices remain without much substance. One example is the injunction that organizations "should maintain as far as possible a consistent methodology of budgetary presentation": the rule does not say which method of presentation is to be preferred, and stipulating that the rule applies "as far as possible" empties it of much of its contents. This was, to a large extent, inevitable: given the wide diversity of organizations and organizational practices it would have been difficult to find any common ground – but in this light, the promulgation of a limited but ambitious set of standards of aspiration might have been more useful.

---

187 The Committee's chair, the seasoned British international lawyer Sir Franklin Berman, noted that the question of the law binding international organizations "was a surprisingly difficult one to answer". The Committee's final report and discussion are reproduced in ILA, *Report of the Seventy-First Conference: Berlin 2004* (2004), 164–241. Sir Franklin's words can be found at p. 238.

However, probably a more relevant reason for the relative disregard for the ILA's work on accountability resides in the emergence of another (if similar enough) approach at roughly the same time: the emergence of GAL.[188] GAL, admittedly, does not focus solely on international organizations, but at the end of the day controlling international organizations is a large chunk of its agenda. More or less simultaneously, scholars working at New York University and at Rome's La Sapienza University noted that international bodies often take decisions that are neither fully comprehensible in terms of classic international law, nor in terms of domestic law. Hence, they envisaged the emergence of a global administrative space, to be filled with GAL, and this GAL is identified not by reasoning from first principles, but by analysing judicial decisions. In doing so, it stays closer to the traditional methodology of international lawyers than the more deductive approach employed by the ILA's Committee on the Accountability of International Organizations, and has been warmly embraced by the international legal community.[189]

Nonetheless, GAL also faces the problem of the basis of legal obligation: much of the global administrative law that has been identified seems to stem from the administrative law traditions of the EU and the US, and may therefore not meet with universal acceptance or approval.[190] And as with some of the ILA's recommended rules and practices, it remains uncertain whether they can be called law, or considered "legally binding" to begin with.[191]

---

188 GAL burst on the scene in 2005 and 2006 with the more or less simultaneous publication of special issues of three respected journals: the *European Journal of International Law*, *Law and Contemporary Problems*, and the *New York University Journal of International Law and Politics*.

189 It has also spawned some related projects, tapping into the same two underlying ideas: wherever public power is exercised, it ought to be subjected to control, and in a pluralist world agreement on what constitutes the proper use of public power is easier to achieve by concentrating on administrative procedure than by focusing on substance. Related works include Nico Krisch, *Beyond Constitutionalism: The Pluralist Structure of Postnational Law* (2010); Benvenisti, *The Law of Global Governance*; and Armin von Bogdandy et al. (eds.), *The Exercise of Public Authority by International Institutions: Advancing International Institutional Law* (2010).

190 Standard critiques along these lines include Carol Harlow, "Global Administrative Law: The Quest for Principles and Values", (2006) 17 *European Journal of International Law* 187–214, and B.S. Chimni, "Co-optation and Resistance: Two Faces of Global Administrative Law", (2005) 37 *New York University Journal of International Law and Politics* 799–827.

191 One of its main proponents has done much to clarify such issues: see Benedict Kingsbury, "The Concept of 'Law' in Global Administrative Law", (2009) 20 *European Journal of International Law* 23–57, and Benedict Kingsbury and Lorenzo Casini, "Global Administrative Law Dimensions of the International Organizations Law", (2009) 6 *International Organizations Law Review* 319–58.

A third approach that has sprung up over the last few decades concentrates on the putative constitutionalization of international organizations. This started, plausibly enough, with attempts to find a vocabulary to describe some of the unique features of the EU, the direct effect and supremacy of EU law in particular.[192] Subsequently it was expanded, however, to cover other organizations as well, and the argument took on three broad dimensions. First, some held that some organizations themselves, most prominently perhaps the WTO, were constitutionalizing, meaning they were in the process of becoming constitutional entities and therewith, so the implication went, bound to respect norms associated with constitutionalism, in particular human rights. Mindful of the trade focus of the WTO, some commentators did not hesitate to proclaim that the relevant human rights included the right to trade and the freedom to contract – here then, constitutionalism took on ordoliberal dimensions.[193]

A second version of the constitutionalization argument suggested that one organizational document in particular, the UN Charter, functions as a global constitution. This particular thesis is usually associated with the work of Bardo Fassbender, and seems intuitively attractive.[194] After all, the UN has a broad and general jurisdiction; the Charter assumes priority over conflicting obligations, and it spans well-nigh all states on the globe. On the other hand, matters are not well-supported by empirical evidence: the privileged position of five member states is difficult to reconcile with any liberal notion of constitutionalism, and surely the lack of attention the Security Council often pays to human rights concerns takes something away from any constitutionalization thesis.

A third variation on the constitutionalization thesis holds that international law generally is going through a process of constitutionalization,

---

192 See Stein, "Lawyers, Judges and the Making of a Transnational Constitution"; Gráinne de Búrca and J.H.H. Weiler (eds.), *The Worlds of European Constitutionalism* (2012).

193 See, for example, Ernst-Ulrich Petersmann, "Time for a United Nations 'Global Compact' for Integrating Human Rights into the Law of World Wide Organizations: Lessons from European Integration", (2002) 13 *European Journal of International Law* 621–50, and Ernst-Ulrich Petersmann, "Human Rights and the Law of the World Trade Organization", (2003) 37 *Journal of World Trade*, 241–81. For a critique, see Jan Klabbers, "Constitutionalism Lite", (2004) 1 *International Organizations Law Review* 31–58; also Deborah Z. Cass, *The Constitutionalization of the World Trade Organization: Legitimacy, Democracy, and Community in the International Trading System* (2005).

194 See Fassbender, *The United Nations Charter*.

with increased attention for fundamental norms, including human rights.[195] Consequently, in order for actors – whether states or organizations or others – to be considered legitimate, their authority must be exercised in accordance with these fundamental norms. Hence, international organizations, as part of this global constitutional structure, can be considered legally bound to respect fundamental norms. Here the inevitable question arises which norms can be considered as fundamental and constitutional, and to the extent that the answer neatly coincides with the Western liberal canon, the thesis lacks persuasive power.[196]

6.5   Skipping legal obligation?

What the ILA's project, GAL, and the constitutionalization thesis have in common is that they all aim to circumvent the problem concerning the basis of legal obligation. It is not clear how international organizations incur legal obligations (other than by their own consent), and as a result it remains unclear how they can be found to be acting in breach of an international legal obligation. And yet, it seems reasonably clear that organizations sometimes do things they should not be doing, or that at least can be seen as controversial. When the World Bank sponsors a project leading to the displacement of thousands of people it seems to be doing something wrong; when the UN fails to intervene during an ongoing genocide, it is doing something wrong; and when NATO is dropping bombs on Belgrade in order to make the Serbian authorities stop ethnic cleansing in Kosovo, it is doing something that is, at least, controversial. Yet, all those activities are difficult to capture in legal terms, and it is no coincidence that commentators have found NATO's intervention over Kosovo possibly to be illegal, yet legitimate.[197]

Where it is unclear whence the law springs, it stands to reason that the perspective shifts towards emphasizing the perceived injustice of the conduct. In technical terms, attention shifts from the basis of legal obligation to the ascription of accountability: those who do wrong

---

195   See for example, Erika de Wet, "The International Constitutional Order", (2006) 55 *International and Comparative Law Quarterly* 51–76.

196   See generally Jan Klabbers, Anne Peters and Geir Ulfstein, *The Constitutionalization of International Law* (2009).

197   See, for example, Bruno Simma, "NATO, the UN, and the Use of Force: Legal Aspects", (1999) 10 *European Journal of International Law* 1–22.

should be called to account even if it remains unclear what exact legal obligations they violate; they should not be allowed to "get away with it".[198]

Sensible as this may sound, the general move to accountability comes with at least two sets of problems. One problem is structural, and holds that in the longer run, the increased focus on accountability and accountability mechanisms may come to lead to a global "audit society", a society where every agency is controlled by a variety of other agencies and trust in those who govern us has largely or completely disappeared.[199] This may not be a very happy state of affairs: the late Ulrich Beck graphically spoke of "McKinsey Stalinism".[200] A global society based on distrust may not be all that pleasant, and there is already anecdotal evidence of international civil servants being "intimidated and paralyzed by audit":[201] if every initiative is subject to close scrutiny, at some point in time initiative will dry up.

Second, and of more immediate practical consequence, is that the very discussion on accountability has made clear that international organizations stand in different accountability relationships with different actors.[202] The World Bank is accountable to its member states: they have every right to insist that the Bank takes its tasks and mandate seriously. Yet the World Bank also stands in a relationship to the people in states where it carries out and sponsors projects, and what is more, different stakeholders will demand performance along different criteria. Surely, the poor and dispossessed in Bangladesh are not too impressed if the World Bank can show that it has followed its instructions from the member states to the letter, while displacing many of Bangladesh's citizens. And this entails that often the Bank will have to compromise in the messy world of everyday politics: between the demands of member states and of the people on the ground; between the desires

---

198 This move to accountability is not limited to situations involving international organizations only: see Jan Klabbers, "From Sources Doctrine to Responsibility? Reflections on the Private Lives of States", in Pierre d'Argent, Béatrice Bonafé and Jean Combacau (eds.), *Les limites du droit international: essais en l'honneur de Joe Verhoeven* (2015), 69–85.

199 See for example, Michael Power, *The Audit Society: Rituals of Verification* (1997), and Onora O'Neill, *A Question of Trust* (2002).

200 See Ulrich Beck, *Nachrichten aus der Weltinnenpolitik* (2010), 67.

201 The phrase was used by a high-ranking UN official during a seminar on the responsibility of international organizations, conducted in May 2013 in Geneva.

202 On the close ties between the IMF and the US Treasury Department, see Randall W. Stone, *Controlling Institutions: International Organizations and the Global Economy* (2011).

of donor states and non-governmental organizations (NGOs); and between the commands of its own constitution and those set by the international community at large. Chances are that no one is entirely happy with the resulting compromise, and the conduct will thus always be vulnerable to criticism.[203]

6.6   Self-control

Given the background of messy politics and the conflicting demands set on international organizations, it is perhaps no coincidence that some of them have started their own internal accountability mechanisms. This is not entirely novel, in that at least since the days of the League of Nations international organizations have been subjected to financial control and auditing. What strikes as rather novel though is that, currently, international auditing mechanisms (and outsourced mechanisms) focus not just on financial control, but also on operational issues.

This self-control takes the form of the appointment of compliance officers, the opening of ethics offices or bureau, the creation of inspection units and the like, and is perhaps most clearly visible within the financial institutions and, to a lesser extent, institutions tasked with security functions.[204] This should not come as a surprise. Historically and conceptually, the topic of ethics in public office is often associated first and foremost with financial issues,[205] and more practically, there is a lot of money circulating around projects sponsored by entities such as the World Bank or the various regional development or investment banks. And where there is a lot of money circulating, there is a high potential for corruption. Moreover, security institutions tend to work in settings where human life is directly at stake. Here, too then, a lot of damage can potentially be done.

Still, self-control may extend beyond purely financial matters. Perhaps the leading example is the work of the World Bank Inspection Panel,

---

203 See generally Friedrich V. Kratochwil, *The Status of Law in World Society: Meditations on the Role and Rule of Law* (2014).

204 For an overview, see Jan Klabbers, "Self-control: International Organisations and the Quest for Accountability", in Malcolm Evans and Panos Koutrakos (eds.), *The International Responsibility of the European Union: European and International Perspectives* (2013), 75–99.

205 Note how the website of the UN Secretary-General comes close to fully equating ethics with financial propriety.

set up in 1993 precisely so as to monitor the operational activities of the World Bank and to help ensure that in its activities, the Bank follows its own procedures and mechanisms. The Inspection Panel can be activated by groups who feel that their rights (or even the rights of others) have been violated by the World Bank in any specific operation. The resulting opinion is non-binding, but may nonetheless send a strong signal to the Bank's management and member states.

While the institutionalization of such self-control mechanisms has become general, sometimes political scandals erupt which demand specific forms of scrutiny. One example is the oil-for-food scandal which embroiled the UN around the turn of the century, prompting the establishment of a committee to enquire into what had happened and whether anyone had done anything wrong. In some circumstances, moreover, ad hoc committees are not so much set up to investigate particular complaints or situations, but rather to address more general dissatisfaction. The UN in particular often makes use of so-called high-level panels to study such things as Security Council reform or peacekeeping.

All of the above examples manifest self-control in one way or another, but all of them also have the potential of fending off external criticism. Subjecting its own policies to the Inspection Panel means that the World Bank can point out that it is doing something about criticism directed at it and is sensitive to societal concerns. Setting up a high-level panel on Security Council reform suggests that the UN is taking such reform seriously. Hence, self-control is both a sword and a shield, and perhaps more shield than sword: it allows the organization to present an image to the world without necessarily doing much about the underlying issues.

7 External relations

7.1 Introduction

Organizations can and do conclude treaties, and generally it is held that whereas the capacity to do so stems from international law, the specific powers needed to conclude specific agreements stem from the organization's constitution. On this line of thinking, all organizations have the capacity to conclude treaties, but whether the FAO can conclude a military agreement depends on the FAO's constituent document.

The specific treaty-making powers, therefore, tend to follow the general discussion on powers as set out above: they are either explicitly conferred, or can be viewed as implied powers. Thus, the UN Charter explicitly envisages the conclusion of treaties between the UN and other international organizations (see articles 57 and 63 of the UN Charter): this is a conferred or attributed power. Less obviously, the UN concludes peacekeeping agreements with states contributing troops: since the UN has no express power to engage in peacekeeping but is generally considered to have an implied power to this effect, it follows that troop-contributing agreements are also based on an implied power.

Even where treaty-making powers are absent, it cannot automatically be concluded that organizations do not enter into treaty relations with other parties. Amongst international lawyers, a popular argument holds that some agreements contain no legal rights or obligations, but merely operate on the political level. On this theory, entities create political commitments which, to be sure, they expect to be respected, but without expecting performance through legal institutions such as courts.[206] It would follow that since no legal relations can be created on the basis of such agreements (often headed Memoranda of Understanding (MoU)), the entity concerned would also not need any

---

206 See generally Anthony Aust, *Modern Treaty Law and Practice* (2nd edn., 2007).

specific powers to enter into them. The ILO, for example, while it has a specific power to conclude treaties with other international organizations and some NGOs (article 12 of the ILO), seems to lack the power to conclude treaties with states; still, its secretariat concludes MoUs with the labour ministries of states.[207]

The idea of there being informal agreements that create no legal obligations but merely political obligations is difficult to sustain on theoretical grounds,[208] and has never been accepted by the ICJ, but nonetheless has become a regular feature of current international law discussions. Terminology is far from straightforward, however. The FAO, for example, which does have an explicit treaty-making power, seems to reserve the term MoU for some of its more serious agreements: it uses MoUs and partnership agreements for high-level cooperation (however, MoU is generally considered the preferred form for agreements without financial ramifications), while Exchanges of letters or Letters of Agreement are used for more fleeting forms of cooperation.[209]

There might be one exception to all this. It could be argued that all organizations have the inherent power to conclude a headquarters agreement, in the sense that the power to do so might be a necessary element of being an international organization, regardless of whether there is an express power to conclude a headquarters agreement, and regardless also of whether such an agreement can be considered necessary in light of any specific function and thus be deemed implied: this seems to be too artificial a construction to have much explanatory power.[210]

Organizations will not only differ in terms of their treaty-making powers (if any), but also with respect to their procedures for treaty-making. It is difficult to say much with any degree of confidence,

---

207 One example concerned cooperation with China, and was concluded in 2001. The text can be found at www.ilo.org/wcmsp5/groups/public/---asia/---ro-bangkok/---ilo-beijing/documents/genericdocument/wcms_144733.pdf (visited 20 January 2015). A more recent example is a MoU concluded with one of India's ministries: www.jagranjosh.com/current-affairs/union-ministry-of-msme-and-ilo-signed-mou-to-support-the-make-in-india-initiative-1415160152-1 (visited 20 January 2015).

208 See Klabbers, *The Concept of Treaty*.

209 See www.fao.org/partnerships/how-to-partner/en/ (visited 20 January 2015).

210 One would otherwise have to argue that concluding a headquarters agreement is necessary for the performance of the functions of the organization, regardless of whether the function is to maintain peace and security, guarantee global health, or stimulate forestry research.

however, as most constituent documents, even those explicitly conferring treaty-making powers, remain silent on the procedure to be followed.

The most active international organization as regards treaty-making is the EU, which is also one of the very few organizations whose constituent document spells out the procedure(s) to be followed.[211] This is not to say that the EU treaty-making procedure is clear: far from it, but at least it is written down. Generally, treaties are negotiated by the Commission, on the basis of instructions from the Council, and approved by the Council. There are important variations, however: matters of peace and security involve the High Representative of the Union for Foreign Affairs and Security Policy, and on a number of issues the consent of the EP is required. The latter requirement serves to protect the legislative powers of the EP, whose approval is required for treaties which may have an impact on those parts of EU law where the EP is co-legislator; otherwise it could be circumvented by means of the conclusion of agreements by the Union.[212] The identity of the persons signing or confirming[213] on behalf of the Union is not mentioned in the treaties; common practice, however, has it that the Council, when adopting the decision to conclude or approve the agreement in question, delegates this task to the Presidency.

In other organizations, the picture is considerably less complicated, and most have no constitutional treaty-making procedure to begin with. Moreover, few other organizations have to take the desires of an organizational parliament into account – or the desires of national parliaments, for that matter. In practice this often means that treaties and other agreements are signed or confirmed by the secretariat. In the UN, for example, consent to be bound is typically expressed by the Secretary-General or a duly authorized plenipotentiary.[214]

---

211 The most recent comprehensive overview of the EU's practice, published well before the Lisbon treaty entered into force, is Delano Verwey, *The European Community, the European Union and the International Law of Treaties* (2004).

212 The main procedure is set out in article 218 TFEU.

213 Confirmation is the equivalent of ratification. In a fit of petty jealousy, the drafters of the 1986 Vienna Convention felt the need to make a distinction between ratification (the sole prerogative of sovereign states) and confirmation: see article 14 1986 Vienna Convention.

214 Sadly perhaps, the most authoritative overview of the UN's treaty practice was written over half a century ago: see Shabtai Rosenne, "United Nations Treaty Practice", (1954/II) 86 *Recueil des Cours* 281–443.

Treaties concluded by an international organization typically come to bind the organization in its entirety: a treaty concluded by the Secretary-General of the UN is not merely binding on the Secretariat, but also binds the General Assembly and the Security Council. The reason for this is that individual organs are thought to lack the required legal personality: the UN is a legal person, its Secretariat is not. As noted though, the binding effect of treaties concluded by an organization does not automatically extend to its member states. The general position would seem to be that member states are considered third parties, and will only be considered bound if three conditions are met: the treaty concerned must be intended to create rights and obligations for the member states; the treaty has been approved by them unanimously, and the treaty partner has been informed. A major exception is formed by EU law, which solves the problem by simply stipulating that agreements concluded by the EU shall bind not just the EU's institutions, but also its member states.[215]

7.2 Mixity

The EU, as alluded to, forms a rather special case when it comes to treaty-making by international organizations. This owes much to the peculiar nature of the EU, which is not merely exercising delegated powers but has, in effect, been granted a number of exclusive powers, to the effect that the member states are pre-empted from acting on their own.[216] The powers of the EU related to international trade and commerce, for example, are deemed to be exclusive – member states are no longer entitled to conclude agreements related to international trade and commerce, and this, in turn, creates an incentive for close cooperation between the Union and its member states when it comes to concluding international agreements with third parties. After all, with many treaties, the situation may arise that a treaty covers matters which are partly the province of exclusive EU powers, and partly still resort under the aegis of the individual member states.

The problem is common to federal states, and several ways have been found to manage the issue. In some states, representatives of the component units may be asked to form part of the team negotiating the

---

215 See article 216(2) TFEU.

216 For a discussion of the international law aspects of the EU, see Jan Klabbers, *The European Union in International Law* (2012).

treaty concerned; in other states, the component units may have a separate chance to formulate their approval or disapproval. In the EU, the cooperation takes the form of "mixity": the conclusion of mixed agreements, heralded by a prominent observer as Europe's "near-unique contribution to true federalism".[217]

The basic idea is simple enough: if a treaty necessitates the participation of both the EU and all or some of its member states, then both the EU and its member states should become parties.[218] A good example is UNCLOS. Most of it deals with matters firmly within the jurisdiction of the EU's member states (such as maritime delimitation), but some parts of it deal with topics that rest within the exclusive competence of the EU: the conservation of marine resources, for instance.

Still, simple as the basic idea is, it can give rise to lots of legal debate. There is, for example, the position of the treaty partner(s) to consider: they might wish to be assured that the obligations contained in the treaty will be performed. Often, therefore, they demand that the EU and its member states issue a statement relating to the precise division of competences between the EU and its member states. Needless to say, the EU is not always very keen on doing this, mostly because it fears that such a statement may carve the current division of competences in stone and make further developments impossible or at least more difficult. Typically then, such statements remain somewhat oblique: the EU declares that "under EU law as it currently stands", the EU assumes responsibility for specific parts and the member states for other specific parts.[219]

Problems may also arise within the EU itself. One issue concerns, for instance, interpretation of the mixed agreement by the CJEU: the CJEU may generally interpret agreements to which the EU is a party, but an argument can be made (and has been made) that it would lack competence over those parts of mixed agreements that would remain within member state prerogatives. To stick to the law of the sea example, the

---

217 See J.H.H. Weiler, *The Constitution of Europe* (1999), 130.

218 The seminal book-length study is Joni Heliskoski, *Mixed Agreements as a Technique for Organizing the International Relations of the European Community and its Member States* (2001). For a useful recent collection, see Christophe Hillion and Panos Koutrakos (eds.), *Mixed Agreements Revisited: The EU and its Member States in the World* (2010).

219 Sometimes the need for mixity is dictated by political considerations. A draft treaty may fall entirely within the scope of EU competence, but participation by the member states through a mixed agreement is thought to enhance the treaty's legitimacy.

CJEU would have jurisdiction to interpret the provisions dealing with conservation of marine resources, but not over those dealing with maritime delimitation. Often, however, the dividing line cannot be drawn with great precision, and the CJEU has a habit of interpreting things in its own favour. Similar problems may arise on a host of other issues. The CJEU has held, for example, that a member state may not introduce new amendments to a treaty on its own: the EU duty of sincere cooperation requires that new amendments may only be proposed by the EU and its member states together.[220]

The CJEU has the power, upon request, to provide advisory opinions on the compatibility of external treaties with EU law.[221] In the 1970s, this power often gave rise to opinions finding that the EU had the required power to join incipient regimes, often based on a version of the implied powers doctrine.[222] In a spate of more recent cases, however, the Court has sometimes ruled that joining a different regime is incompatible with EU law. It tends to do so in particular when the overarching treaty provides for its own judicial institution and even gives it a superior ranking: this would mean that in joining, the EU would subject itself to another court, and this, the CJEU has repeatedly held, is incompatible with EU law, in particular the provision that the CJEU shall be the guardian of legality in the EU.[223] On this basis, the CJEU has, for instance, rejected the EU's participation in a European Patent Court[224] and, most recently, rejected the negotiated treaty on accession of the EU to the ECHR.[225]

Membership by the EU of other international organizations mostly creates legal issues on the receiving end, so to speak: the organization that the EU wants to join must be open to EU participation – in the early 1990s, the FAO amended its constitution in order to facilitate EU membership. Moreover, the organization concerned must figure out how to treat the EU in the budgetary process (should the EU be separately assessed, in addition to its member states, or rather to some extent replace its member states?) and when it comes to voting. Within

---

220 See Case C-246/07, *Commission* v. *Sweden* [2010] ECR I-3317.
221 See article 218(11) TFEU.
222 See, for example, *Opinion 1/76* [1977] ECR 754.
223 See article 19 TEU.
224 See *Opinion 1/09* [2011] ECR I-1137.
225 See *Opinion 2/13* of 18 December 2014 (nyr). See also Jan Klabbers, "On Myths and Miracles: The EU and Its Possible Accession to the ECHR", (2013) 1 *Hungarian Yearbook of International and European Law* 45–62.

the EU, provision must be made on who gets to speak within another organization and on which topics (when do the member states speak, and when does the EU speak). Within the WTO, with its robust and active dispute settlement mechanism, third parties may have to decide in case of conflict whether to bring a claim against the EU or against one or several of its member states.[226]

7.3 Inter-organizational relations

Sociologists and legal sociologists have observed, over the last few decades, that social relations increasingly fragment into specific social sectors. Authority is no longer exercised solely by territorially based states, but is increasingly organized around particular functions.[227] Thus, they distinguish a security regime from the educational sector, and distinguish a health regime from the realm of economics. In many of these regimes, key roles are performed by international organizations. These, after all, were set up (at least in theory) around the idea of a specific function. The WHO, by this standard, plays an important role in the global health regime, but it is not the only important player. Important roles are also reserved for the pharmaceutical industry, for NGOs such as Médecins Sans Frontières, and for philanthropist institutions such as the Bill and Melinda Gates Foundation.[228]

The upshot of this type of argument is not just that authority is organized along lines of "functional differentiation", but also that the various regimes end up both competing and cooperating with one another.

The competition between regimes has received plenty of attention amongst international lawyers in the form of a long-standing preoccupation with what became known as the fragmentation of international law.[229] If international law fragments into a security regime,

---

226 See generally Martin Björklund, "Responsibility in the EC for Mixed Agreements – Should Non-member Parties Care?", (2001) 70 *Nordic Journal of International Law* 373–402.

227 Many of the examples in this section and the next are culled from Jan Klabbers, *An Introduction*, ch. 13.

228 See, for example, Gunther Teubner, *Constitutional Fragments: Social Constitutionalism and Globalization* (2012).

229 See, for example, Joost Pauwelyn, *Conflict of Norms in Public International Law: How WTO Law Relates to Other Rules of International Law* (2003); Andreas Fischer-Lescano and Gunther Teubner, *Regime-Kollisionen: Zur Fragmentierung des globalen Rechts* (2006); Martti

a trade regime, an environmental regime, and so on, then how should conflicts between those regimes, or between norms emanating from these regimes, be solved or mitigated? Concretely, if a trade rule collides with an environmental rule, then how should actors act? Additionally, there have been discussions on the role of courts and the scope of their jurisdictions, focusing on questions whether it would be possible, or even desirable, to have trade courts sit in judgment of environmental matters or human rights.[230]

Competition between international organizations is most acutely visible on the regional and ideological levels. The establishment of the EU prompted some other European states to set up the European Free Trade Area (EFTA), and stimulated the USSR to create the COMECON. Military alliances such as NATO may provoke the creation of other military alliances (Warsaw Pact), and the predominance of Western-style liberalism has no doubt contributed to the formation of the OIC. It is, indeed, in the nature of things that closed organizations, precisely by aiming to protect the interest of their members, can only do so by competing with others. The same applies to attempts to cooperate between regional entities: by definition, including some amounts to excluding others.

Finally, it is no coincidence that currently the so-called BRICS[231] are instrumental in setting up institutions that can challenge Western dominance, including an investment bank to rival existing investment banks.[232] A number of tax havens, moreover, have established the International Trade and Investment Organization (ITIO) in order to offer an alternative to the OECD and its attempts to regulate taxation globally.[233]

Where regime conflicts and fragmentation have been widely discussed, cooperation between and within functional regimes has slipped somewhat below the radar screen. Still, even cooperation amongst

---

Koskenniemi, *Fragmentation of International Law: Difficulties Arising from the Diversification and Expansion of International Law. Report of the Study Group of the International Law Commission* (2007); and Jan Klabbers, *Treaty Conflict and the European Union* (2009).

230 The leading study in this genre is Yuval Shany, *The Competing Jurisdictions of International Courts and Tribunals* (2003).

231 The acronym stands for Brazil, Russia, India, China and South Africa.

232 See http://rt.com/business/198928-china-world-bank-rival/ (visited 28 January 2015).

233 The ITIO is briefly discussed in Peter Carroll and Aynsley Kellow, *The OECD: A Study of Organizational Adaptation* (2011), 142.

international organizations alone has a long tradition, and is increasingly widespread. The underlying reason for such cooperation will be obvious: even if it is possible to designate some issues as "health issues", for example, few issues do not spill over into other issue areas. Thus, health issues are connected to medication, which immediately involves the trade and intellectual property regimes. Health issues can be approached from human rights angles (right to health, right to life), and can thus involve the human rights regime. If ill people go travelling, the health regime may intersect with, in particular, the aviation regime, and in some cases, moreover, even the security regime may become involved: the outbreak of epidemics and pandemics may generate movement of people across borders to such an extent that neighbouring states might start to feel threatened. Hence, while functional differentiation takes place, the functional regimes cannot exist in a vacuum.[234]

Connections between international organizations can take several forms. A first is through the formal linking of membership and of organizations. States can only join the World Bank if they are already members of the IMF, and joining the ILO is easier for UN members than for non-members. And under article 57 of the UN Charter, a number of international organizations are brought together in the "UN family": the entities so brought together include the WHO, WIPO, the ILO, the FAO and the World Meteorological Organization (WMO). Altogether, it involves 15 international organizations and the sprawling World Bank group, which itself comprises a number of entities. These are often referred to as the "specialized agencies", with the name suggesting that while the UN itself exercises a general jurisdiction, these individual organizations have a more specialized function, and together they constitute something of a world government.[235] Other organizations have also entered into a relationship with the UN, but are not considered to form part of the UN family in quite the same way. This applies, amongst others, to the WTO and the OPCW.

---

234 See generally Jeffrey L. Dunoff, "A New Approach to Regime Interaction", in Margaret Young (ed.), *Regime Interaction in International Law: Facing Fragmentation* (2012), 136–74; and Jeffrey L. Dunoff, "Is Sovereign Equality Obsolete? Understanding Twenty-first Century International Organizations", (2012) 43 *Netherlands Yearbook of International Law*, 99–127.

235 The ICJ tried to further develop this idea in *Legality of the Use by a State of Nuclear Weapons in Armed Conflict*, advisory opinion, [1996] ICJ Reports 66, but the result was less than plausible. For commentary, see Jan Klabbers, "Global Governance before the ICJ: Re-reading the WHA Opinion", (2009) 13 *Max Planck Yearbook of United Nations Law* 1–28.

The example of the World Bank group suggests that international organizations can be involved in the creation of a number of other entities with related tasks. The World Bank has created the International Development Association (IDA) and the International Finance Corporation (IFC) to provide different kinds of loans to member states in need, and has created the Multilateral Investment Guarantee Agency (MIGA) and the International Centre for the Settlement of Investment Disputes (ICSID) in order to facilitate and protect investments in poorer countries.

The UN itself has created the UNIDO in the 1960s as a programme – it became an independent organization (and a specialized agency) in 1985.

If organizations can inspire the creation of new organizations on their own, they can also do so together. The most well-known form of joint venture between two organizations is perhaps the WFP, set up in the early 1960s between the UN and the FAO. The FAO also set up, together with the WHO, the Codex Alimentarius Commission, a body tasked with setting food safety standards, while the World Bank, together with two UN programmes (the environmental programme, UNEP, and the development programme, UNDP) helped set up the Global Environmental Facility (GEF) in 1991. A number of organizations, moreover, set up the Inter-Organization Programme for the Sound Management of Chemicals in 1995. These included the WHO, the OECD and UNIDO, and the Joint Vienna Institute was even created as a formal international organization solely by a number of existing international organizations.

There exist also other, more ad hoc, forms of cooperation between organizations. The ITU and ICAO are helping each other in studying how mobile phones and similar devices can be used onboard aircraft without interfering with navigations systems; officials at the FAO and the WTO are discussing fisheries issues; while WTO and ILO officials look at linkages between trade and labour and WTO and UNEP officials focus on linkages between trade and environmental concerns.[236]

Traditionally, regional organizations have sometimes been placed at the service of universal organizations,[237] most prominently in connection

---

236 The examples are derived from Dunoff, *A New Approach*.
237 See generally Laurence Boisson de Chazournes, "Les relations entre organisations regionales et organisations universelles", (2010) 347 *Recueil des Cours* 83–406.

with peace and security issues. Thus, it is not unusual for the UN to ask for the help of regional organizations to help solve regional conflicts, and sometimes regional organizations themselves offer their help, either in their own region or elsewhere. NATO has engaged in policing tasks on behalf of the UN in Kosovo and Afghanistan, while the EU volunteered to take part in actions in various African countries. Both NATO and the EU, moreover, take part in the work of the Contact Group on Piracy off the Coast of Somalia, as does an organization such as IMO.

The UN Charter even envisages a formal relationship between the UN and regional organizations in article 53, but this has been less successful than hoped for. Part of the reason may be that such a formal relationship entails obligations: it might mean that the regional organization feel less at liberty to act without UN support, and at any rate the regional organization undertakes some reporting obligations. For this reason, NATO has always been reluctant to view itself as an "article 53" organization.[238]

A nice example is also that the G20 has asked the OECD to prepare a set of rules covering the situation where large companies engage in "tax planning" to such an extent that they hardly pay any taxes at all: in jargon, this is referred to as "base erosion and profit shifting". To this end, the OECD is actively considering the almost unprecedented technique of sponsoring the conclusion of a multilateral agreement to amend a large number of existing bilateral agreements on taxation.[239]

Yet another form of cooperation takes place not so much (or not solely) on the operational level, but on the administrative level, with one organization hosting another and performing administrative tasks on the latter's behalf. Perhaps the leading example is that the International Union for the Protection of New Varieties of Plants (UPOV) is housed in WIPO's premises and administered by the latter.

In such situations, complicated questions of legal responsibility can arise, as a 2012 advisory opinion of the ICJ suggests. The International Fund for Agricultural Development (IFAD) had for a number of years administered the secretariat of the convention establishing a global

---

238 See Sarooshi, *The United Nations and the Development of Collective Security* 251.
239 See www.oecd.org/tax/beps-about.htm (visited 22 January 2015). The technique of using a multilateral agreement to amend sets of bilateral agreements is rare, but not entirely new: perhaps the leading earlier example is the 1957 European Convention on Extradition.

mechanism to combat desertification. The contract of one of the employees of the latter was not renewed, leading the staff member concerned to contest the lawfulness of her dismissal before the relevant administrative tribunal (ILOAT) by starting proceedings against IFAD. IFAD claimed that since she was an employee of the global mechanism secretariat, IFAD was not involved in any wrongdoing, but ILOAT disagreed and found in the applicant's favour. Subsequently, IFAD asked for an ICJ opinion, and the ICJ by and large agreed with the applicant and ILOAT, arguing that IFAD had assumed responsibility for the administration of the global mechanism secretariat. Indeed, communications on the matter had been done on official IFAD paper, and the applicant had been listed as an IFAD employee for the purposes of receiving immunities and privileges. Hence, IFAD had been far more than a mere clearing house.[240]

7.4   Public-private partnerships

International organizations do not only set up all sorts of partnership with each other, but also, increasingly, with the private sector. Some of this is born out of sheer necessity. Some of the better-known programmes (UNHCR, WFP) receive little or no compulsory member state contributions, and are thus fully dependent on voluntary contributions. These may stem from states (the US is by far the single largest contributor to UNHCR's budget, followed at quite some distance by Japan, the EU, Sweden and the Netherlands), but can also come from the corporate sector: in 2012 UNHCR received some 20 million dollars from the IKEA Foundation. A Dutch lottery chipped in with a little over 3 million dollars, and even the football club AC Milan contributed, albeit with the relatively small sum (given the amount of money circulating in world football) of 194,000 dollars.[241] Sometimes the corporate sector contributes in kind rather than financially: Coca-Cola has allowed its refrigerated trucks to be used for the transportation of vaccines for the WHO in sub-Saharan Africa.

Apart from the necessity of cooperating with the private sector for financial reasons, international organizations have also been affected

---

240 See *Judgment No. 2867 of the Administrative Tribunal of the International Labour Organization upon a Complaint Filed Against the International Fund for Agricultural Development*, advisory opinion, [2012] ICJ Reports 10.

241 See www.unhcr.org/pages/49c3646c26c.html (visited 22 January 2015).

by the popularity of neo-liberal thought (one would be tempted to speak of ideology) that market-based solutions are often deemed superior to public action. Especially the WHO has been pioneering the establishment of a number of newly fashioned entities. These include public-private partnerships in the field of global health, such as the GAVI Alliance (vaccines and immunization), which brings together the WHO, the Bill and Melinda Gates Foundation and others, but also an entity such as UNAIDS, a conglomerate of a number of organizations.[242]

Such public-private partnerships also feature on other topics, however, being prominently visible on topics such as water (the Global Water Partnership[243]), education (the Global Partnership for Education), or forestry (the Collaborative Partnership on Forests). Such entities provoke a number of legal (and political) questions, relating for instance to their governance, and in particular to questions of responsibility: if an entity such as the GAVI Alliance causes damage, which of the participating entities can be held responsible, and on the basis of which standards?[244]

---

242 See Gian Luca Burci, "Public/Private Partnerships in the Public Health Sector", (2009) 6 *International Organizations Law Review*, 359–82.

243 For a useful overview, see Edouard Fromageau, "The Global Water Partnership: Between Institutional Flexibility and Legal Legitimacy", (2011) 8 *International Organizations Law Review*, 367–95.

244 Even single authors can propose different conclusions. Thus, in different writings, Clarke has endorsed the applicability of state responsibility and of the responsibility of participating international organizations. See Lisa Clarke, "Global Health Public-Private Partnerships: Better Protecting Against Disease but Creating a Gap in Responsibility under International Law", (2009) 20 *Finnish Yearbook of International Law*, 349–72; and Lisa Clarke, "Responsibility of International Organizations under International Law for the Acts of Global Health Public-Private Partnerships", (2011) 12 *Chicago Journal of International Law*, 55–84.

8 Re-thinking the law of international organizations

The law of international organizations developed in the late nineteenth and early twentieth century through the works of scholars like Jellinek, Kazansky, Reinsch and Sayre, and quickly became dominated by the approach they advocated: functionalism. The underlying idea (and justification for organizations) was that organizations were assigned specific functions; this made them worthwhile entities, operating beyond politics, and entailed that a body of legal rules and doctrines could and should be developed so as to facilitate their functioning.

Those halcyon days quickly passed. Already after the First World War, when functionalism had just been established, the most prominent newly created organizations did not fit functionalism's blueprint. The League of Nations lacked a specific function, instead, it had a large array of functions. And the ILO's main function was to fend off the communist danger by helping to improve the working man's plight and implicating him (and to a lesser extent her) in decision-making regarding his own situation.[245] Hence, functionalism lived on, but came to be applied to all sorts of actors for whose tasks and structures it was not developed and for whom it was, really, rather inappropriate.

It took a while to notice, but by the 1960s the cracks in functionalism's edifice started to show. Property owners started to complain about their properties being damaged during UN operations, but functionalism could not provide a satisfactory answer. It could only insist on the functional immunity of the UN and tinkering a bit at the margins by allowing for minor claims to be settled. Employees of organizations started to complain not just about being passed over for promotion, but also about discrimination and harassment by their superiors. Again, functionalism could not think of a principled answer other than allowing organizations to set up internal complaint mechanisms in the form of administrative tribunals.

---

245 See further Jan Klabbers, "The Transformation".

And two decades later, it turned out that some of functionalism's problems were structural. The 1980 WHO–Egypt opinion underlined the ambivalent position of member states embroiled in a dispute with their own organization; the drafting of the 1986 Vienna Convention on the Law of Treaties Concluded with or Between International Organizations suggested that the position of member states with respect to treaties concluded by their organization is problematic; and the insolvency of the International Tin Council made clear that the responsibility of organizations towards third parties was outside the scope of functionalism. Furthermore, as organizations developed their operational activities, it was precisely on matters of responsibility and accountability that the limits of functionalism were most clearly felt.

Functionalism had, and still has, meaningful things to say about the relationship between organizations and their member states. Even if functionalism has problems coming to terms with the idea that an organization's functioning is always subject to political influences, nonetheless it can help explain why organizations have powers, why they have privileges and immunities, why they can set conditions for membership, or why members are under an obligation to help finance the organization.

Functionalism is not able to explain all that happens.[246] It cannot account for political interventions; why some member states have been suspended for human rights violations rather than their prowess in contributing to the organization's function; why some organizations have broader privileges and immunities than others; or why some organizations have more functions than others. But even if it cannot provide a total explanation, it can provide helpful insights.

What functionalism cannot do, however, is say anything about how the organization works internally (relations between organs and with staff), and how it can and should operate towards the outside world. In other words, functionalism has something to say about issues arising out of the relationship between the organization and its members, but has nothing to contribute on aspects of international organizations that do not directly involve the relationship with the member states.

Yet, it is precisely to these issues that attention has shifted, in a somewhat paradoxical way. The more organizations undertake operational

---

246 It can explain the functional, but not the dysfunctional. I am indebted to Mikael Rask Madsen for helping me to sharpen the point.

activities, the less relevant the ties to their member states become. Put graphically, when the UN administered territory in Kosovo, the chance of it doing something that would affect the life of the inhabitants of Kosovo was far greater than the chance that any action undertaken in Kosovo would directly come to affect, say, Botswana. When UNHCR runs a refugee camp in Kenya, its activities there will affect individual refugees rather than, say, Norway. Hence, the more active the organization becomes, the more it comes to affect individual lives, and the less (at least in relative terms) does it come to affect its member states. This may be, to some extent, an overstatement, in that, earlier, organizations could come to affect individuals as well, but those effects were often indirect, mediated by those very same member states.

If all this is plausible and the trend towards operational activities proves irreversible, then it follows that functionalism has little to offer for the future of the law of international organizations beyond the insight that it may be beneficial for the world at large if the work of some organizations can be facilitated by the legal structures of international organizations law. But this will demand a re-conceptualization of the very notion of international organization. There is little justification for allowing cartels such as OPEC or interest groups such as the EU or the OIC to work without interference and control: such benefits as accrue to organizations under functionalism should be reserved to those that serve the global common good in one way or another. And while some might say (with considerable justification perhaps) that all universal projects are particular projects clothed in universalist garb,[247] others might still feel that perhaps entities such as UNICEF or the WHO cannot be reduced to merely endorsing particular interests.

In addition, for functionalism to continue to contribute, those applying it must do so in modesty and remain faithful to the idea of functionalism. This suggests, quite simply, that the task of the WHO is to help provide for global health; its function is not to expand its own bureaucracy or jurisdiction. It suggests that the task of the IOM is to help relieve the plight of migrants; it is doubtful whether operating migrant processing centres on behalf of states helps contribute much to this task. In short, mission creep can only be fought by those who are actually engaged in the mission: it takes a certain kind of attitude on

---

247 As Carl Schmitt put it evocatively, "whoever invokes humanity wants to cheat". See Carl Schmitt, *The Concept of the Political* (1996 [1932], Lomax trans.), 54.

the part of the leadership of international organizations to make them work in accordance with functionalist thought.[248]

Beyond this, though, the discipline must look elsewhere for inspiration, and has indeed started to do so. Discussions on the relations between organs of organizations and on such topics as judicial review tend to be informed by constitutional theory or, more broadly perhaps, public law theory, rather than functionalism. And for good reason, of course: the question whether the ICJ can review acts of the Security Council cannot be solved in a meaningful way by functionalism; the functionalist could only point to the function of the Council, and conclude that nothing should interfere with the functioning of the Council, and thus judicial review is anathema. But that ignores precisely the fact that the call for judicial review stems from dissatisfaction with the way the Council functions. Much the same applies to staff disputes involving charges of harassment or discrimination: relying on functionalist immunity is largely beside the point. Likewise, functionalist thought is unlikely to help much in figuring out how to organize relations with the outside world. In a treaty dispute between the EU and Japan, for example, it will hardly be persuasive to argue that the functioning of the EU warrants special consideration.

Alternatively, a different kind of functionalism may be considered, where it is not the functioning of any individual organization which occupies centre stage, but rather the functioning of the globe at large. This would have the advantage at least of allowing various interests to factor into the equation: a broader notion of functionalism could entail that the World Bank not just be accountable to its member states, but also to the poor and dispossessed. This, however, may well remain a pipe dream, as it presupposes the sort of shared theory of justice which, in a pluralist and divided world, is lacking.

In the meantime, at least two trends are discernible. First, there seems to be a growing convergence involving the law on immunities, staff relations, and issues of accountability, manifested by decisions such as

---

248 See, very briefly, Jan Klabbers, "Controlling International Organizations: A Virtue Ethics Approach", (2011) 8 *International Organizations Law Review* 285–9, and Jan Klabbers, "Autonomy, Constitutionalism and Virtue in International Institutional Law", in Richard Collins and Nigel D. White (eds.), *International Organizations and the Idea of Autonomy: Institutional Independence in the International Legal Order* (2011), 120–40.

Waite and Kennedy.[249] Here, the three legal dynamics identified above come together: such issues involve the relationship between organization and member states, as well as internal relations and external relations. This alone would call for a re-thinking of the theory underlying the law of international organizations, and suggests that functionalism on its own may lack explanatory force and, at the same time, lead to results that would be difficult to embrace.

Second, one of the central hallmarks of functionalism, the proposition that organizations exercise their function in accordance with specific powers, may be seen to be resting on untenable assumptions. Perhaps the main assumption is the idea that powers belong either to the state or to the organization, but this has proved to be questionable. At the very least, it is possible that states acting under their own powers come to encroach on the powers of the organization, and vice versa: organizations acting within their powers may nonetheless encroach on the powers supposedly retained by their member states. This is an inherent element of all functionalist thinking: functions can be separated analytically, but in practice often overlap.[250] The power to occupy itself with global health, so central to the WHO, will at some point intersect with the power to set rules for the pharmaceutical industry. Giving one to an organization while retaining the other means that the borderline between the two will need to be policed, and this is a difficult, perhaps impossible task. It is no coincidence then that, in practice, organizations engage in relations with each other, with states, and with other actors, and can do so by not taking precise power conferrals all that seriously. In the EU this is even codified: while the EU can boast some exclusive powers, on some topics its powers are explicitly meant to be "complementary" to those of member states,[251] or "support and complement" those of member states.[252]

---

249 See *Waite and Kennedy*, discussed in Chapter 2 section 2.5.

250 Ironically perhaps, this insight was central to another theory labelled functionalism. Functionalist integration theory assumed that cooperation in one field would (almost) automatically spill over into other sectors. Something approaching a manifesto is David Mitrany, "The Prospect of Integration: Federal or Functional", (1965) 4 *Journal of Common Market Studies* 119–49.

251 See for example, article 168 TFEU on public health; article 180 TFEU on research and development; article 195 TFEU on tourism; article 208 TFEU on development cooperation; or article 214 TFEU on humanitarian aid.

252 See article 196 TFEU on civil protection. See generally Jan Klabbers, "Restraints on the Treaty-Making Powers of Member States Deriving from EU Law: Towards a Framework for Analysis", in Enzo Cannizzaro (ed.), *The European Union as an Actor in International Relations* (2002) 151–75.

At the end of the day, regardless of the doubts one may entertain about specific organizations or the way the various functionalist doctrines operate, there remains something worth cherishing about international organizations: if they did not exist, they ought to be invented. It may be too much to expect organizations to single-handedly arrange for the "salvation of mankind", as one prominent observer phrased his hopes in the late 1950s.[253] But salvation of mankind or not, international organizations, warts and all, have come to symbolize mankind's hopes. Today the world may be a bad place, but tomorrow's world may be better. As Oscar Wilde reportedly once said, a map of the world without a place for Utopia is not worth looking at.[254]

---

253 See Nagendra Singh, *Termination of Membership of International Organisations* (1958), vii.

254 See Rosemary Righter, *Utopia Lost: The United Nations and World Order* (1995), ix.

Bibliography

Alford, William P., "The Prospective Withdrawal of the United States from the International Labor Organization: Rationales and Implications", (1976) 17 *Harvard International Law Journal* 623–38.

Alvarez, José E., *International Organizations as Law-makers* (2005).

Alvarez, José E., "Legal Remedies and the United Nations' à la Carte Problem", (1991) 12 *Michigan Journal of International Law* 229–311.

Amerasinghe, C.F., *Principles of the Institutional Law of International Organizations* (2nd edn., 2005).

Annan, Kofi with Nader Mousavizadeh, *Interventions: A Life in War and Peace* (2012).

Asamoah, Obed Y., *The Legal Significance of the Declarations of the General Assembly of the United Nations* (1966).

Ascensio, Hervé and Nicola Bonucci (eds.), *Le pouvoir normatif de l'OCDE* (2013).

Aust, Anthony, *Modern Treaty Law and Practice* (2nd edn., 2007).

Barnett, Michael and Martha Finnemore, *Rules for the World: International Organizations in Global Politics* (2004).

Bass, Gary J., *Stay the Hand of Vengeance: The Politics of War Crimes Tribunals* (2000).

Beck, Ulrich, *Nachrichten aus der Weltinnenpolitik* (2010).

Bederman, David J., *Custom as a Source of Law* (2010).

Beigbeder, Yves, *Management Problems in United Nations Organizations: Reform or Decline?* (1987).

Bekker, P.H.F., *The Legal Position of Intergovernmental Organizations: A Functional Necessity Analysis of their Legal Status and Immunities* (1994).

Benvenisti, Eyal, *The Law of Global Governance* (2014).

Björklund, Martin, "Responsibility in the EC for Mixed Agreements – Should Non-member Parties Care?", (2001) 70 *Nordic Journal of International Law* 373–402.

Blokker, Niels M., "Is the Authorization Authorized? Powers and Practice of the UN Security Council to Authorize the Use of Force by 'Coalitions of the Willing'", (2000) 11 *European Journal of International Law* 541–68.

Blokker, Niels M., "International Organizations and their Members", (2004) 1 *International Organizations Law Review* 139–61.

Bogdandy, Armin von et al. (eds.), *The Exercise of Public Authority by International Institutions: Advancing International Institutional Law* (2010).

Boisson de Chazournes, Laurence, "Les relations entre organisations régionales et organisations universelles", (2010) 347 *Recueil des Cours*, 83–406.

Bölingen, Stefan, *Die Transformation der NATO im Spiegel der Vertragsentwicklung: Zwischen sicherheitspolitischen Herausforderungen und völkerrechtlicher Legitimität* (2007).

Brölmann, Catherine M., "The 1986 Vienna Convention on the Law of Treaties: The History of Draft Article 36*bis*", in Jan Klabbers and René Lefeber (eds.), *Essays on the Law of Treaties: A Collection of Essays in Honour of Bert Vierdag* (1998), 121–40.

Brölmann, Catherine M., *The Institutional Veil in Public International Law: International Organisations and the Law of Treaties* (2007).

Broms, Bengt, *The Doctrine of Equality of States as Applied in International Organizations* (1959).

Buergenthal, Thomas, *Law-making in the International Civil Aviation Organization* (1969).

Bühler, Konrad, *State Succession and Membership in International Organizations: Legal Theories versus Political Pragmatism* (2001).

Búrca, Gráinne de and J.H.H. Weiler (eds.), *The Worlds of European Constitutionalism* (2012).

Burci, Gian Luca, "Public/Private Partnerships in the Public Health Sector", (2009) 6 *International Organizations Law Review* 359–82.

Cane, Peter, *Responsibility in Law and Morality* (2002).

Carroll, Peter and Aynsley Kellow, *The OECD: A Study of Organizational Adaptation* (2011).

Cass, Deborah Z., *The Constitutionalization of the World Trade Organization: Legitimacy, Democracy, and Community in the International Trading System* (2005).

Castaneda, Jorge, *Legal Effects of United Nations Resolutions* (1969).

Chesterman, Simon (ed.), *Secretary or General? The UN Secretary-General in World Politics* (2007).

Chimni, B.S., "Co-optation and Resistance: Two Faces of Global Administrative Law", (2005) 37 *New York University Journal of International Law and Politics* 799–827.

Chinkin, Christine, *Third Parties in International Law* (1993).

Clarke, Lisa, "Global Health Public-Private Partnerships: Better Protecting Against Disease but Creating a Gap in Responsibility under International Law", (2009) 20 *Finnish Yearbook of International Law* 349–72.

Clarke, Lisa, "Responsibility of International Organizations under International Law for the Acts of Global Health Public-Private Partnerships", (2011) 12 *Chicago Journal of International Law* 55–84.

Cogan, Jacob Katz, "Representation and Power in International Organization: The Operational Constitution and Its Critics", (2009) 103 *American Journal of International Law* 209–63.

Craig, Paul and Gráinne de Búrca, *EU Law: Text, Cases and Materials* (5th edn., 2011).

Craven, Matthew, "Legal Differentiation and the Concept of the Human Rights Treaty in International Law", (2000) 11 *European Journal of International Law* 489–520.

Curtin, Deirdre, *Executive Power of the European Union: Law, Practices, and the Living Constitution* (2009).

Daugirdas, Kristina, "Reputation and the Responsibility of International Organizations", (2014) 25 *European Journal of International Law* 991–1018.

Davies, Gareth, "Subsidiarity: The Wrong Idea, In the Wrong Place, At the Wrong Time", (2006) 43 *Common Market Law Review* 63–84.

Descamps, Edouard Baron, *Les offices internationaux et leur avenir* (1894).

Dugard, John, *Recognition and the United Nations* (1987).

Dunoff, Jeffrey L., "A New Approach to Regime Interaction", in Margaret Young (ed.), *Regime Interaction in International Law: Facing Fragmentation* (2012), 136–74.

Dunoff, Jeffrey L., "Is Sovereign Equality Obsolete? Understanding Twenty-first Century International Organizations", (2012) 43 *Netherlands Yearbook of International Law*, 99–127.

Duxbury, Alison, *The Participation of States in International Organisations: The Role of Human Rights and Democracy* (2011).

Eagleton, Clyde, "International Organization and the Law of Responsibility", (1959/I) 76 *Recueil des Cours* 319–425.

Elias, T.O., "Modern Sources of International Law", in Wolfgang Friedmann et al. (eds.), *Transnational Law in a Changing Society: Essays in Honor of Philip C. Jessup* (1972), 34–69.

Engström, Viljam, *Constructing the Powers of International Institutions* (2012).

Farrall, Jeremy Matam, *United Nations Sanctions and the Rule of Law* (2007).

Fassbender, Bardo, *The United Nations Charter as the Constitution of the International Community* (2009).

Feichtner, Isabel, *The Law and Politics of WTO Waivers: Stability and Flexibility in Public International Law* (2012).

Fischer-Lescano, Andreas and Gunther Teubner, *Regime-Kollisionen: Zur Fragmentierung des globalen Rechts* (2006).

Footer, Mary E., *An Institutional and Normative Analysis of the World Trade Organization* (2006).

Fröhlich, Manuel, *Political Ethics and the United Nations: Dag Hammarskjöld as Secretary-General* (2008).

Fromageau, Edouard, "The Global Water Partnership: Between Institutional Flexibility and Legal Legitimacy", (2011) 8 *International Organizations Law Review*, 367–95.

Grant, Thomas D., *Admission to the United Nations: Charter Article 4 and the Rise of Universal Organization* (2009).

Harlow, Carol, "Global Administrative Law: The Quest for Principles and Values", (2006) 17 *European Journal of International Law* 187–214.

Helfer, Laurence R., "Nonconsensual International Lawmaking", (2008) *University of Illinois Law Review* 71–125.

Heliskoski, Joni, *Mixed Agreements as a Technique for Organizing the International Relations of the European Community and its Member States* (2001).

Hillion, Christophe and Panos Koutrakos (eds.), *Mixed Agreements Revisited: The EU and its Member States in the World* (2010).

Howland, Douglas, "An Alternative Mode of International Order: The International Administrative Union in the Nineteenth Century", (2015) 41 *Review of International Studies* 161–83.

ILA, *Report of the Seventy-First Conference: Berlin 2004* (2004).

Jacob, Gregory F., "Without Reservation", (2004) 5 *Chicago Journal of International Law* 287–302.

Johnstone, Ian, *The Power of Deliberation: International Law, Politics and Organizations* (2011).

Katz, Jonathan M., *The Big Truck That Went By: How the World Came to Save Haiti and Left Behind a Disaster* (2013).

Kazansky, Pierre, "Théorie de l'administration internationale", (1902) 9 *Revue Générale de Droit International Public* 352–66.

Keith, Kenneth J., *The Extent of the Advisory Jurisdiction of the International Court of Justice* (1971).

Kennedy, David, "The Move to Institutions", (1987) 8 *Cardozo Law Review* 841–988.

Kennedy, Paul, *The Parliament of Man: The Past, Present, and Future of the United Nations* (2006).

Kingsbury, Benedict, "The Concept of 'Law' in Global Administrative Law", (2009) 20 *European Journal of International Law* 23–57.

Kingsbury, Benedict, and Lorenzo Casini, "Global Administrative Law Dimensions of the International Organizations Law", (2009) 6 *International Organizations Law Review* 319–58.

Kingsbury, Benedict, Nico Krisch, and Richard Stewart, "The Emergence of Global Administrative Law", (2005) 68 *Law and Contemporary Problems*, 15–61.

Klabbers, Jan, *The Concept of Treaty in International Law* (1996).

Klabbers, Jan, "Presumptive Personality: The European Union in International Law", in Martti Koskenniemi (ed.), *International Law Aspects of the European Union* (1998), 231–53.

Klabbers, Jan, "The Changing Image of International Organizations", in Jean-Marc Coicaud and Veijo Heiskanen (eds.), *The Legitimacy of International Organizations* (2001), 221–55.

Klabbers, Jan, "The Life and Times of the Law of International Organizations", (2001) 70 *Nordic Journal of International Law* 287–317.

Klabbers, Jan, "Restraints on the Treaty-Making Powers of Member States Deriving from EU Law: Towards a Framework for Analysis", in Enzo Cannizzaro (ed.), *The European Union as an Actor in International Relations* (2002), 151–75.

Klabbers, Jan, "Constitutionalism Lite", (2004) 1 *International Organizations Law Review* 31–58.

Klabbers, Jan, "The *Bustani* Case before the ILOAT: Constitutionalism in Disguise?", (2004) 53 *International and Comparative Law Quarterly* 455–64.

Klabbers, Jan, "Straddling Law and Politics: Judicial Review in International Law", in R.St.J. MacDonald and D.M. Johnston (eds.), *Towards World Constitutionalism* (2005), 809–35.

Klabbers, Jan, "Two Concepts of International Organization", (2005) 2 *International Organizations Law Review* 277–93.

Klabbers, Jan, "Checks and Balances in the Law of International Organizations", in Mortimer Sellers (ed.), *Autonomy in the Law* (2007), 141–63.

Klabbers, Jan, "The Paradox of International Institutional Law", (2008) 5 *International Organizations Law Review* 151–73.

Klabbers, Jan, "Global Governance before the ICJ: Re-reading the WHA Opinion", (2009) 13 *Max Planck Yearbook of United Nations Law* 1–28.

Klabbers, Jan, "Lawmaking and Constitutionalism", in Jan Klabbers, Anne Peters and Geir Ulfstein, *The Constitutionalization of International Law* (2009), 81–125.

Klabbers, Jan, *Treaty Conflict and the European Union* (2009).

Klabbers, Jan, "Reflections on the Politics of Institutional Reform", in Peter Danchin and Horst Fischer (eds.), *United Nations Reform and the New Collective Security* (2010), 76–93.

Klabbers, Jan, "Autonomy, Constitutionalism and Virtue in International Institutional Law", in Richard Collins and Nigel D. White (eds.), *International Organizations and the Idea of Autonomy: Institutional Independence in the International Legal Order* (2011), 120–40.

Klabbers, Jan, "Controlling International Organizations: A Virtue Ethics Approach", (2011) 8 *International Organizations Law Review* 285–9.

Klabbers, Jan, "International Courts and Informal International Law", in Joost Pauwelyn, Ramses A. Wessel and Jan Wouters (eds.), *Informal International Lawmaking* (2012), 219–40.

Klabbers, Jan, *The European Union in International Law* (2012).

Klabbers, Jan, *International Law* (2013).

Klabbers, Jan, "On Myths and Miracles: The EU and Its Possible Accession to the ECHR", (2013) 1 *Hungarian Yearbook of International and European Law* 45–62.

Klabbers, Jan, "Self-control: International Organisations and the Quest for Accountability", in Malcolm Evans and Panos Koutrakos (eds.), *The International Responsibility of the European Union: European and International Perspectives* (2013), 75–99.

Klabbers, Jan, "Unity, Diversity, Accountability: The Ambivalent Concept of International Organisation", (2013) 14 *Melbourne Journal of International Law* 149–70.

Klabbers, Jan, "Marginalized International Organizations: Three Hypotheses Concerning the ILO", in Ulla Liukkunen and Chen Yifeng (eds.), *China and ILO Fundamental Principles and Rights at Work* (2014), 181–96.

Klabbers, Jan, "The Emergence of Functionalism in International Institutional Law: Colonial Inspirations", (2014) 25 *European Journal of International Law* 645–75.

Klabbers, Jan, *An Introduction to International Organizations Law* (3rd edn., 2015).

Klabbers, Jan, "From Sources Doctrine to Responsibility? Reflections on the Private Lives of States", in Pierre d'Argent, Béatrice Bonafé and Jean Combacau (eds.), *Les limites du droit international: essais en l'honneur de Joe Verhoeven* (2015), 69–85.

Klabbers, Jan, "Intervention, Armed Intervention, Armed Attack, Threat to Peace, Act of Aggression and Threat or Use of Force: What's the Difference", in Marc Weller (ed.), *The Oxford Handbook on the Use of Force in International Law* (2015), 488–506.

Klabbers, Jan, "The EJIL Foreword: The Transformation of International Organizations Law", (2015) 26 *European Journal of International Law*, 9–82.

Klabbers, Jan, "Theorising International Organisations", in Florian Hoffmann and Anne Orford (eds.), *The Oxford Handbook of International Legal Theory* (forthcoming).

Klabbers, Jan, Anne Peters, and Geir Ulfstein, *The Constitutionalization of International Law* (2009).

Kolb, Robert, *An Introduction to the Law of the United Nations* (2010).

Koskenniemi, Martti, *Fragmentation of International Law: Difficulties Arising from the Diversification and Expansion of International Law. Report of the Study Group of the International Law Commission* (2007).

Kratochwil, Friedrich V., *The Status of Law in World Society: Meditations on the Role and Rule of Law* (2014).

Krisch, Nico, *Beyond Constitutionalism: The Pluralist Structure of Postnational Law* (2010).

Kunz, Joseph, "Privileges and Immunities of International Organizations", (1947) 41 *American Journal of International Law* 828–62.

Lagrange, Evelyne and Jean-Marc Sorel (eds.), *Traité de droit des organisations internationales* (2013).

Liivoja, Rain, "The Scope of the Supremacy Clause of the United Nations Charter", (2008) 57 *International and Comparative Law Quarterly* 583–612.

Lowe, A.V., *International Law* (2007).

Lukes, Steven, *Power: A Radical View* (1974).

MacMillan, Margaret, *Paris 1919: Six Months that Changed the World* (2003).

Magliveras, Konstantinos D., *Exclusion from Participation in International Organisations: The Law and Practice behind Member States' Expulsion and Suspension of Membership* (1999).

Masson-Mathee, Mariëlle, *The Codex Alimentarius Commission and Its Standards* (2007).

Mazower, Mark, *Governing the World: The History of an Idea* (2012).

Mégrét, Frédéric, "La responsabilité des Nations Unies aux temps du choléra", (2013) *Revue Belge du Droit International* 161–89.

Mendelson, Maurice, "Reservations to the Constitutions of International Organizations", (1971) 45 *British Yearbook of International Law* 137–71.

Mitrany, David, "The Prospect of Integration: Federal or Functional", (1965) 4 *Journal of Common Market Studies* 119–49.

Muller, A.S., *International Organizations and their Host States* (1995).

Murphy, Craig N., *International Organization and Industrial Change: Global Governance Since 1850* (1994).

Myers, Patrick R., *Succession between International Organizations* (1993).

Nicholas, H.G., *The United Nations as a Political Institution* (3rd edn., 1967).

Oakeshott, Michael, *On Human Conduct* (1975).

Obradovic, Daniela, "Repatriation of Powers in the European Community", (1997) 34 *Common Market Law Review* 59–88.

O'Neill, Onora, *A Question of Trust* (2002).

Orford, Anne, *International Authority and the Responsibility to Protect* (2011).

Paulus, Andreas, "Article 29", in Bruno Simma et al. (eds.), *The Charter of the United Nations: A Commentary* (3rd edn., 2012), 987–1027.

Pauwelyn, Joost, *Conflict of Norms in Public International Law: How WTO Law Relates to Other Rules of International Law* (2003).

Peters, Anne and Simone Peter, "International Organizations: Between Technocracy and Democracy", in Bardo Fassbender and Anne Peters (eds.), *The Oxford Handbook of the History of International Law* (2012), 170–97.

Petersmann, Ernst-Ulrich, "Time for a United Nations 'Global Compact' for Integrating Human Rights into the Law of World Wide Organizations: Lessons from European Integration", (2002) 13 *European Journal of International Law* 621–50.

Petersmann, Ernst-Ulrich, "Human Rights and the Law of the World Trade Organization", (2003) 37 *Journal of World Trade*, 241–81.

Power, Michael, *The Audit Society: Rituals of Verification* (1997).

Ragazzi, Maurizio (ed.), *Responsibility of International Organizations: Essays in Memory of Sir Ian Brownlie* (2013).

Reinalda, Bob, *Routledge History of International Organizations: From 1815 to the Present Day* (2009).

Reinisch, August, *International Organizations before National Courts* (2000).

Reinsch, Paul S., *Public International Unions, Their Work and Organization: A Study in International Administrative Law* (1911).

Righter, Rosemary, *Utopia Lost: The United Nations and World Order* (1995).

Röling, B.V.A. and Antonio Cassese, *The Tokyo Trial and Beyond* (1993).

Rosenne, Shabtai, "United Nations Treaty Practice", (1954/II) 86 *Recueil des Cours* 281–443.

Rosenne, Shabtai, "Is the Constitutional Instrument of an International Organization an International Treaty?", in Shabtai Rosenne, *Developments in the Law of Treaties 1945–1986* (1989), 181–258.

Ruffert, Matthias and Christian Walter, *Institutionalisiertes Völkerrecht* (2009).

Sands, Philippe and Pierre Klein, *Bowett's Law of International Institutions* (6th edn., 2009).

Sarfaty, Galit A., *Values in Translation: Human Rights and the Culture of the World Bank* (2012).

Sarooshi, Dan., *The United Nations and the Development of Collective Security: The Delegation by the UN Security Council of its Chapter VII Powers* (1999).

Sarooshi, Dan, *International Organizations and their Exercise of Sovereign Powers* (2005).

Sato, Tetsuo, *Evolving Constitutions of International Organizations* (1996).

Sayre, Francis B., *Experiments in International Administration* (1919).

Schermers, H.G., and Niels M. Blokker, *International Institutional Law: Unity Within Diversity* (5th edn., 2011).

Schmalenbach, Kirsten, *Die Haftung internationaler Organisationen* (2004).

Schmitt, Carl, *The Concept of the Political* (1996 [1932], Lomax trans.).

Seyersted, Finn, *Objective International Personality of Intergovernmental Organizations: Do their Capacities Really Depend on the Conventions Establishing Them?* (1963).

Seyersted, Finn, *Common Law of International Organizations* (2008).

Shany, Yuval, *The Competing Jurisdictions of International Courts and Tribunals* (2003).

Simma, Bruno, "NATO, the UN, and the Use of Force: Legal Aspects", (1999) 10 *European Journal of International Law* 1–22.

Sinclair, Guy F., "State Formation, Liberal Reform, and the Growth of International Organizations", available at http://papers.ssrn.com/sol3/papers.cfm?abstract_id=2545767.

Singer, Michael, "Jurisdictional Immunity of International Organizations: Human Rights and Functional Necessity Concerns", (1995) 36 *Virginia Journal of International Law*, 53–165.

Singh, Nagendra, *Termination of Membership of International Organisations* (1958).

Stein, Eric, "Lawyers, Judges, and the Making of a Transnational Constitution", (1981) 75 *American Journal of International Law* 1–27.

Stone, Randall W., *Controlling Institutions: International Organizations and the Global Economy* (2011).

Tammes, A.J.P., "Decisions of International Organs as a Source of International Law", (1958/II) *Recueil des Cours* 265–363.

Teubner, Gunther, *Constitutional Fragments: Social Constitutionalism and Globalization* (2012).

Tuytschaever, Filip, *Differentiation in European Union Law* (1999).

Tzanakopoulos, Antonios, *Disobeying the Security Council: Counter-measures against Wrongful Sanctions* (2011).

Veitch, Scott, *Law and Irresponsibility: On the Legitimation of Human Suffering* (2007).

Verdirame, Guglielmo, *The UN and Human Rights: Who Guards the Guardians?* (2011).

Verwey, Delano, *The European Community, the European Union and the International Law of Treaties* (2004).

Virally, Michel, "La notion de fonction dans la théorie de l'organisation internationale", in Suzanne Bastid et al. (eds.), *Mélanges offerts à Charles Rousseau: La communauté international* (1974), 277–300.

Weiler, J.H.H., "Alternatives to Withdrawal from an International Organization: The Case of the European Economic Community", (1985) 20 *Israel Law Review* 282–98.

Weiler, J.H.H., *The Constitution of Europe* (1999).

Wet, Erika de, "The International Constitutional Order", (2006) 55 *International and Comparative Law Quarterly* 51–76.

Williams, Paul R., "State Succession and the International Financial Institutions: Political Criteria v. Protection of Outstanding Financial Obligations", (1994) 43 *International and Comparative Law Quarterly* 766–808.

Williams, Susan, *Who Killed Hammarskjöld? The UN, the Cold War and White Supremacy in Africa* (2013).

Wittich, Stephan, "Permissible Derogation from Mandatory Rules? The Problem of Party Status in the Genocide Case", (2007) 18 *European Journal of International Law* 591–618.

Woods, Ngaire, *The Globalizers: The IMF, the World Bank, and Their Borrowers* (2006).

Yemin, Edward, *Legislative Powers in the United Nations and Specialized Agencies* (1969).

Zacklin, Ralph, *The Amendment of the Constitutive Instruments of the United Nations and Specialized Agencies* (1968).

Index